Through the Fire

To the Stirling,
Thank you for
your love &
care.
Love
Janice

Through the Fire

A MIRACULOUS JOURNEY

Janice E. Harris

THROUGH THE FIRE by Janice E. Harris

This book is non-fiction. It is an account of actual experiences that I had during my cancer journey and other times in my life. For information contact Janice Harris at godchaser1922@aol.com

All Scripture quotations are from the King James Version of the Bible, unless otherwise specified.

Cover designed by Stephen Edward Griffin
Library of Congress Control Number: 2017917479

First Edition: 2017

ISBN: 0692979212
ISBN 13: 9780692979211

Printed in the United States of America

Dedication

I dedicate this book to my dear mother, Mrs. Marian E. Harris, who passed away shortly before my cancer journey began. She taught me many valuable lessons and demonstrated to me what faith could do in a person's life. She was also a cancer survivor for many years, and a woman of extreme faith and love.

Contents

Acknowledgments

To all my family and friends who helped me in any way throughout my journey, I thank you. There are too many of you to name. I am so grateful that the Lord placed people in my life, who have mentored and encouraged me to stand even when I didn't know if I could make it to the next step. All of you are very special to me.

A special thanks to Reverend Dr. Robin Vickers, Mr. Stephen Griffin, Ms. Marian Elesha Richardson and Mrs. Cassie Dandridge Selleck for your contributions to this book.

Foreword

In this inspiring book, you will find a chronicle of events about a long-time friend who was diagnosed with sarcoma cancer. She is alive today and tells details of her journey from beginning to end, as well as other life experiences. It is the five-year mark from the date of surgery to remove the cancerous tumor — and she has the victory.

More importantly, as author of this book, she tells a great and inspiring lesson that what's impossible with man is possible with God, and to never give up.

During those five years, I witnessed a Christian friend's endurance, faith, and praise in the midst of the fire. I also witnessed the trials and tests that she had to go through, and how she overcame this devastating experience.

Minister Janice Harris is an inspiration and cancer survivor. To God be the glory for all He has done in her life. What a remarkable journey to be remembered!

Rev. Dr. Robin Vickers

First Lady, New Vision Christian Center Ministries
Hallandale Beach, Florida

Adjunct College Professor
Miami-Dade and Broward County

Introduction

The word "fire" is used in many ways, especially throughout the Bible. All of us can identify with this word in one way or another. As a child, we were taught not to play with fire as it could result in danger. Fire can burn or consume anything it encounters. Unless you are using a fire to warm yourself up, cook, light up a space or any other productive purpose, it is not usually dealt with.

Even though we speak often of a literal fire, the word "fire" is also used symbolically. In the Word of God, it could mean God's judgment, a start of a conflict, or a description for God himself—as in the very presence of God demonstrated in the pillar of fire that led the Israelites. There is also fire related to Hell, the burning bush in the story of Moses, and other examples.

In this book, my use of the word "fire" relates to the trials and tribulations that Christians and others go through in their lives. We all have certainly been in or through a fire, which is different for each of us. Just like fires have varying degrees of heat, so do the fires in our lives.

The challenge for us as Christians is not if we will have a fire experience but how we will go through it and continue to stand for Christ when the tests of life are over.

I pray that as you read this book you will be encouraged to stand amid any trial that you face in your life, and that you will grow closer to the God who created you and me.

I consider my battle with cancer the biggest "fire experience" in my life. I am aware that there are many different beliefs as to why a Christian experiences sickness and disease. I am a believer that sickness can be a result of sin, a satanic attack, carelessness with our eating habits, etc. However, I am also a believer according to the scriptures, that there are times when God uses sickness to get the glory out of someone's life.

In 2012, I received a miracle from God that changed my life forever. It is my prayer that my personal testimonies will inspire you to be a light to others who may be struggling to understand why God has allowed them to go through the fiery trials in their lives. I assure you that in the midst of it all, God loves you unconditionally.

1

The News

I don't know of anyone who loves to hear bad or unpleasant news, no matter how big or small the matter is. Bad news resounds in one's ear like a projectile being fired from a cannon.

Have you ever experienced a telephone call, letter, text or some other means of communication about something you just did not expect to hear? That news may have been life altering, or something that had a minor effect on you or someone you love. The news may have knocked you off your feet—like swimming in an ocean with gigantic waves rippling through the water, knocking down every unwilling victim.

Many of us consider ourselves to be good, but after receiving such news, the first thought or question we ask is, "What have I done wrong?" Although we have learned that our goodness does not prevent unpleasant things from happening, we are still caught off guard when things go awry in our lives. In some situations, we filter questions in our minds reflecting on how we have lived our lives.

We sometimes allow our past, which may be good, bad or ugly, to flash before us like watching the change of scenes in a movie. These are ways in which we tend to measure whether we are deserving of major occurrences that have happened in our lives. Honestly speaking, even though many of us have encouraged others who were dealing with difficult situations, we find it hard to understand when we are faced with similar problems.

I have definitely experienced some of these thoughts. In early January of 2012, I received some shocking news at a hospital located in Pembroke Pines, Florida. I had gone to its emergency room due to several weeks of pain in my right leg, the hamstring area. The pain had started after I felt a small elongated bump under the skin, which looked and felt a little unusual to me. In my mind, this bump may have been the result of a near fall off my home treadmill about a week before it appeared. I thought I may have pulled or strained a muscle.

While in the ER, the house doctor told me I would be admitted for further testing and observation. I felt relieved that I was getting closer to finding out what was going on because the pain was worsening by the day. Also, the growing bump was causing me a lot of discomfort sitting and sleeping because of where it was located.

The Beginning

The issue started in December of 2011. Early that month, I had traveled to a friend's college graduation in Louisiana. While traveling, I experienced a lot of pain in my hamstring area, which made it very difficult to drive. I had no idea what was happening, so I applied an over the counter arthritis ointment to the area. Instead of getting better, the pain got worse during the trip. I returned home from the trip determined to find out what was wrong, but I did not seek medical attention immediately.

It was then time to travel for the Christmas holiday, and I was concerned about taking another trip in this condition. Therefore, on the way out of town I visited the ER at a hospital in Miami, Florida. I was given an ultrasound to determine if there were any blood clots in my leg. I was relieved at the news that I had no clots. The ER doctor at this first hospital told me that maybe I had strained a muscle. He discharged me with advice to see an orthopedic and to take muscle relaxing medication.

I then drove over 200 miles to my hometown for Christmas. The drive was difficult because I continued to experience pain. Over the holidays, I struggled to enjoy myself despite all the pain and discomfort. I knew that when I returned to Miami, I would have to follow-up on this issue.

After I returned, I followed the instructions of the ER doctor at the Miami hospital, and made a visit to my personal orthopedic. He diagnosed the problem as a hematoma (a solid swelling of clotted blood within the tissues), and sent me for a MRI at a local center to confirm his findings. Both his and the center's diagnoses matched, and confirmed a hematoma.

The normal procedure after a MRI is to return to the doctor who ordered the test to go over the findings. Instead of returning to that doctor, it was now January of 2012 and I was lying in a hospital bed in a completely different hospital. I was waiting for a doctor to go over the results of a new MRI that had been ordered. I will explain more on that later.

God Prepares Us

I have always felt something spiritual within me that I knew was much bigger than myself. As a young girl, I started having dreams that seemed to be prophetic, although I did not have a clue what was happening to me. I have always felt the ability to discern when something was good to do or if it was bad idea.

Growing up, I had said the "Sinner's Prayer" many times in the summer when a group of missionaries set up shop in a local community church to teach children about Christ. This was in addition to what I had already learned in my regular church, Sunday school, Bible study, etc.

I learned a lot about Christ during those summer sessions. Those dedicated missionaries made learning fun for me, my siblings, as well as some of the other children in the community. I still remember the songs we sang, such as the *"Good News"* song. I can still hear the words ringing in my ears:

> Good News! Good News!
> Christ died for me
> Good News! Good News!
> If I believe
> Good News! Good News!
> I'm saved eternally
> That's wonderful
> EXTRA Good News!

I can also remember watching movies about Christ, which always made me feel warm inside. On the other hand, the movies also made me uncomfortable with the fact that I had a long way to go to be like the Man, the Christ, whom I was seeing in the movies.

Altar calls to receive salvation was a large part of those summer meetings. I can reflect on those days, seeing many of us walking slowly to the altar accepting Christ in our lives. I did not fully understand this act that I was taking part in, but I knew I wanted to be more like Jesus, so I took these altar calls very seriously.

However, once the missionaries had left town and public school started again, I was faced with the same dilemma as usual, which was how to live differently than before. I also toiled with the decision to tell my friends that I felt different. I knew that God was touching me in some way, but I felt I had to keep it to myself, at least until I knew what to do with it.

Lord I Need An Answer

Yes, growing up I felt that Jesus was speaking to me in many different situations. In many ways, His speaking to me about the pain in my leg was no different. Even though the first hospital ER doctor in Miami had not found anything in December, my orthopedic had diagnosed me with a hematoma, and the initial MRI had confirmed the hematoma, there was still a quiet voice within me saying very clearly that *something was not right!*

That same quiet voice would not allow me to sleep peacefully at night. At the same time, that horrible pain was keeping me awake! I could not shake the feeling that there was more to it. Lying in bed one night I heard these words in my spirit, "Janice, do not go back to the orthopedic for the results of the MRI; do not waste time with that."

Over the years after giving my life completely to Christ, I had come to recognize when the Holy Spirit was guiding me. There were times when I heard the Holy Spirit speak so clearly, and then times when I just felt an unction to do something.

During my employment years with the state of Florida, one of my job duties was to act as a liaison for human rights committees appointed by the Governor. I set up meetings and audits for them. One committee planned to do an audit of facilities in Key West, Florida. I was scheduled to conduct a meeting prior to the audit, and was to fly to Key West early on the morning of the meeting.

I scheduled a taxi to pick me up and transport me to the Miami International Airport (MIA). Unfortunately, the taxi arrived late to my home and by the time I arrived to the airport my airplane had already departed. Dismayed, I sat in the airport waiting for the next flight which would get me to my destination after my meeting was scheduled to start.

I was very distressed over the situation. I sat there praying for God to help me, as it would not be a good thing for me to be late. Suddenly, I heard these words clearly in my spirit, "Don't worry. Joanie will also be late, and she will come and make a way for you to get to your meeting on time." I was astounded, and I was very sure it was the Holy Spirit that had spoken to me, but the likelihood of someone else being late seemed very slim to me.

I sat there for about thirty minutes or more still puzzled. Suddenly, to my amazement, Joanie walked in. Just as the Holy Spirit had said, Joanie had also missed her flight. She was full of smiles as if she was oblivious to the situation at hand. She said to me "Oh Janice you missed the plane too. Don't worry we will get there on time." I looked at her in total wonderment. "How could she be so sure about getting us anywhere on time?" I thought. Joanie had always been a very spunky woman.

She asked me to come along as she headed over to the check-in desk of a totally different airline. I watched and listened as she began to negotiate with the customer service agent at the desk. Not only was the agent there, but the owner of the small airline (ten seater) was also standing at the desk. He announced that he was about to fly to Key West and that we were welcomed to switch our service to his airline.

I was speechless! Within minutes we were on the plane and headed to Key West. More importantly, we arrived on time for me to conduct the meeting. These are the types of experiences I have had in my life. I knew first-hand that God could speak to me, and that He could also answer my prayers.

Regarding this pain in my leg, I also felt that I was being guided by the Holy Spirit, even though I had no idea why. Therefore, I planned late during the night while I lay awake in pain, to go to a different hospital the next morning to seek understanding of what was going on in my body.

In early January of 2012, I lay in the bed at the new hospital and waited for the doctor to walk in to deliver the results of the new MRI. I had no idea what that news would be. I was just trusting my God that he would tell me I could go home, and was hoping that he would provide me with a prescription for pain and/or other medication to resolve the issue.

It was Sunday morning there in the hospital when I was watching the news regarding a female track star who had a sarcoma cancerous tumor on her leg, and medical procedures had taken her out of circulation as a runner for some time. However, the story told of her triumph over this ugly disease called "cancer" and she had just successfully completed and won a race. Yes, she won. She beat the odds and survived.

I found this to be such a heartwarming story. Until that moment, I had never heard of sarcoma cancer, but I was so happy for this person whom I did not even know. Little did I know that I was about to become very familiar with the word "SARCOMA".

No matter how spiritual you are or how many things you have experienced in life, you never feel fully prepared for some storms or "fires" that you will encounter. Although we may not realize it, God is always preparing us. The question we must ask ourselves is, "Have we been listening and following His instructions?"

One scripture that will help us to be prepared is Ephesians 6:13-18.

Wherefore take unto you the whole armour of God, that ye may be able to withstand in the evil day, and having done all, to stand. Stand therefore, having your loins girt about with truth, and having on the breastplate of righteousness;
And your feet shod with the preparation of the gospel of peace;
Above all, taking the shield of faith, wherewith ye shall be able to quench all the fiery darts of the wicked.
And take the helmet of salvation, and the sword of the Spirit, which is the word of God:
Praying always with all prayer and supplication in the Spirit, and watching thereunto with all perseverance and supplication for all saints;

If we have been dressing daily in our spiritual garments, we can better handle all the fiery darts. Not only have I always taken pride in being an encouragement to others, but I have always been told that I am a strong Christian woman known for uplifting others.

More importantly, I have always taken the above scripture to heart and have considered myself a praying woman, an intercessor, and one who has dressed daily in the whole armor to the extent possible. Nevertheless, situations in my life have challenged my faith in God.

Yes, I thought I was prepared for the news that the doctor was about to deliver to me that day in January, but it was about to be a fire that would light up every part of my being and alter my life forever. It is clear now that those prayers and church activities throughout my past and current life were about to help me through much more than I knew was to come.

The Diagnosis

I have always hated going to doctors. I am a person who despises watching medical television shows, or anything having to do with medical procedures. I am always nervous about any diagnosis that I could possibly be given. Like many other people, my imagination would go wild, which made my situations seem even more difficult.

The doctor walked in and stood at my bedside. He began to speak to me gently, but with a lot of confidence that the news he was delivering was very accurate. He started by apologizing for my extended stay in the hospital, which was supposed to be overnight, but had lasted several days.

He explained that the previous MRI that I had taken at the MRI center, per my regular orthopedics' orders, was not a very good reading because it was done on an open MRI machine. He also explained that those machines do not take the best images. Yes, I acknowledge the fact that I purposely chose an open MRI because I had never had the courage to go into the regular machine.

During my conversation with the doctor, I had a sinking feeling that began to flow through my body from head to toe. My mind was running a mile a minute, and I tried to imagine what the doctor would say next. I asked myself "Will he say that the results are better than the previous MRI diagnosis, or worse?" I felt like screaming to him— sir, please get to the point!

He continued to explain that he was the lead orthopedic on staff at the hospital. I had been treated several times at this hospital in the past, and have always given high marks for its excellent service. However, I wondered if this was going to be the first time that I would be disappointed.

The doctor seemed to be building himself up by telling me how good he was. He said even the hospital staff often sought him out for orthopedic treatment and advice. I am sure he was just trying to ensure me that I was in good hands, but his delay was causing me to wonder if this news would be okay. He finally told me that he was very sure about the information he was about to provide!

And then there it was, the words that I was totally not expecting. He said in a very sympathetic tone, "Ms. Harris, the lump on your hamstring is not a hematoma. I am very sure it is a sarcoma cancerous tumor." He went on to explain that this was a rare cancer that attacks the soft muscle tissue. "We have done all we can do for you here, and now I will refer you to the top doctors at the University of Miami Hospital (UMHC), who can treat you with the best of care," he said.

Oh my God, why me? This question hit my mind like a sudden strong wind fiercely swaying the branches of a tree from side to side. It totally caught me off guard. Yes, I had been feeling in my spirit that it was something more than the initial orthopedic had told me, but I had certainly not thought of this!

If I had never been at a loss of words, this was the time! I had no family or anyone in the room to help me digest this awful news. I had told a few people that I was going to the hospital, and they all knew I had been admitted, but none of them would have expected this outcome.

God Was Already There!

Again, this was on a Sunday morning. I had awakened early that morning in the hospital room with one of my favorite songs playing in my head. The song "I Give Myself Away" found its way to my lips as I lay there singing softly to myself.

The words had been ringing in my head all morning. *"I give myself away so you can use me."* I had sung this song many times, but maybe I did not really focus on what it was saying. I did know that I wanted God to use me, but I was now asking myself, "What does this situation have to do with God using me?"

I had texted my pastor, Reverend Warnell A. Vickers, of New Vision Christian Center in Hallandale, Florida. I learned that at the time this song fell in my spirit, our church praise team was singing the same song. That morning so far had been very inspirational for me, as I even watched a church service on television.

None of this could calm my mind during the time the doctor was speaking to me. All I could think was where was God? Why was I hearing this information? All my mind could process at that time was how this had to be a terrible mistake. I didn't care how prominent this doctor was, nor what credentials he had; this could not be further from the truth.

No, this was not a fire that I was ready or willing to go through at this point in my life. I said to myself, "God, this is surely a test of my faith! This cannot be happening now, God. Heavenly Father, you must come through and prove that all the doctor just said is a huge mistake!" I was waiting for God to answer me. After all, I had always been assured that I was His child! Yes, His child! I could hear this scripture sounding loud in my spirit:

Psalm 28:1

Unto thee will I cry, O LORD my rock; be not silent to me: lest, if thou be silent to me, I become like them that go down into the pit.

2

In The Fire

As children, some of us have read familiar Bible stories such as Daniel in the Lion's Den or The Three Hebrew men, Shadrach, Meshach and Abednego who were thrown in the fire. How many of us can consider that we have had a "fire" experience? Though your experiences may not have been as dramatic as some accounts in the Bible, they are not less spiritual or less important.

In the story of the Hebrew men, they were thrown in a literal fire. God used their situation to encourage and inspire us that no matter what we are facing — He will be right there to see us through. However, sometimes when we are in the fire we may not fully realize what God is doing. This certainly does not lessen the fact that we are being used for something greater than we know. In the book of Daniel, the trial that these young men went through was as dramatic as most would imagine.

Daniel 3:20-30
And he commanded the most mighty men that were in his army to bind Shadrach, Meshach, and Abednego, and to cast them into the burning fiery furnace.
Then these men were bound in their coats, their hosen, and their hats, and their other garments, and were cast into the midst of the burning fiery furnace.

Therefore because the king's commandment was urgent, and the furnace exceeding hot, the flames of the fire slew those men that took up Shadrach, Meshach, and Abednego.

And these three men, Shadrach, Meshach, and Abednego, fell down bound into the midst of the burning fiery furnace.

Then Nebuchadnezzar the king was astonished, and rose up in haste, and spake, and said unto his counsellors, Did not we cast three men bound into the midst of the fire? They answered and said unto the king, True, O king.

He answered and said, Lo, I see four men loose, walking in the midst of the fire, and they have no hurt; and the form of the fourth is like the Son of God.

Then Nebuchadnezzar came near to the mouth of the burning fiery furnace, and spake, and said, Shadrach, Meshach, and Abednego, ye servants of the most high God, come forth, and come hither. Then Shadrach, Meshach, and Abednego, came forth of the midst of the fire.

And the princes, governors, and captains, and the king's counsellors, being gathered together, saw these men, upon whose bodies the fire had no power, nor was an hair of their head singed, neither were their coats changed, nor the smell of fire had passed on them.

Then Nebuchadnezzar spake, and said, Blessed be the God of Shadrach, Meshach, and Abednego, who hath sent his angel, and delivered his servants that trusted in him, and have changed the king's word, and yielded their bodies, that they might not serve nor worship any god, except their own God.

Therefore I make a decree, That every people, nation, and language, which speak any thing amiss against the God of Shadrach, Meshach, and Abednego, shall be cut in pieces, and their houses shall be made a dunghill: because there is no other God that can deliver after this sort.

Then the king promoted Shadrach, Meshach, and Abednego, in the province of Babylon.

Just as God allowed these men to be thrown into the flames for His glory, He will also allow us to be thrown or led into the fire to make us better, and allow others to see Christ in us. The men went in the fire seemingly alone, yet God Almighty was with them.

As much as I have read and believed this story, I still could not fully understand why I had to go through cancer. I wondered what good this would be to me or even my family. However, I have learned that when we are in the fire, we'll find out what is in us. Sometimes we have no idea how strong we are until we go through certain tests. The three Hebrew men came out of the fire with evidence of their dependence and faith in the Almighty God.

When I received the diagnosis from the hospital doctor, I knew to even digest what he was saying — I had to believe that there was something inside of me strong enough to help me make it through if it turned out to be true. However, at that time I did not believe for one minute that this information was accurate. It's not that I mistrusted the doctor, rather I believed that he was human and could have made a mistake.

What Now?

My dilemma started in early December of 2011, and I was now in a hospital in early January of 2012. Prior to that, in June of 2011 my family had just experienced the loss of my sister Pearl, who was two years older than I. Two months later we experienced the loss of our eighty-eight-year-old mother who not only had been a survivor of lung cancer for almost twenty years, but was also a walking and living testimony to God's grace and favor.

Mom was a devout Christian woman who never smoked one day in her life. As a matter of fact, she had never entered a night club or any other environment where she would have been affected by second-hand smoke. Doctors at the Moffitt Cancer Center in Tampa, Florida were amazed at her survival and state of health for such a long time.

She was often asked by doctors what she did daily. Her response was, "I cook, clean, do laundry and perform many other chores." Interestingly, they were often astonished at this petite woman who did not show any outward signs of lung cancer at all even though she had surgeries to remove affected parts of her lungs, and had been on a chemotherapy pill during her last years.

In early 2011, my mother's speech began to slur. Shortly after, we took her to her doctor and was informed that the cancer had metastasized to her brain. In a matter of weeks, she went from a healthy-looking woman to frail.

News of my sister Pearl's sudden sickness took a further toll on mom. After a lengthy hospital stay, Pearl's health declined. Before that, she had improved well enough to go to a nursing home, but one night she was found unresponsive and was admitted to the hospital again and never recovered. In fact, the family decided to remove her from life support.

It was a difficult time for my siblings and me when we had to explain to our mother, who was in her last days, that Pearl had passed. Mother's health declined rapidly after that and we chose to have the hospice services in her own home, which we knew she would want. Sadly, she passed away in August of 2011.

My sister and mother's death had devastated our family. My mother delivered seventeen children and one died at birth which still left sixteen from two marriages (twelve from my father). I was born the thirteenth child. At the time of my sister and mother's death, we had already lost a set of twin adult brothers, Daniel and David, in two separate tragic accidents.

Therefore, when the hospital doctor gave me the news that I had cancer, I sat on the hospital bed screaming within myself "Lord why would you allow me and my family to go through something else like this so soon?" I repeated to myself over and over after the doctor walked out of the room, "Lord what now?" I heard nothing but silence, yet I felt a knowing in my spirit that God was there.

Yes, I had seen devastation, but I had also seen how God moved in other's lives. I even had my own share of testimonies of God's healing and miraculous power over the years. Yet somehow, I was not feeling very triumphant at the time the doctor was giving me the news, or for days after.

I was now in a fire that would change my life forever. I was in a fight for my life. I had taken days off my job to help care for my mother in her last days. I had cried more tears than I had done in my entire life. I had watched my mother breathe her last breath and take her peaceful transition from this earth. I believed that she was with the Lord. She had taken care of so many people in her lifetime, always going about doing good.

My mom was known for going to neighbors' homes when they were sick, and cleaning or feeding them if needed. She taught me the principle of giving and helping others. I had comforted many others in their time of need. Now I was in a battle of faith, and a war against the enemy of my soul.

I was discharged from the hospital that day in early January, devastated, but believing that God would work the situation out. I did not know how, when, or under what circumstances, but I understood that I had been a Born-Again Christian for over thirty years and I knew something about God's grace and mercy. I knew that the Word of God says in 2 Chronicles 20:15, "for the battle is not yours, but God's." That was enough to give me the strength to make it through the coming days and nights.

God Is Our Refuge

During your troubles and situations, this scripture is very uplifting. I read it during the time of my trouble, and I continue to read this when I need an encouraging word.

Psalm 91: 1-16

He that dwelleth in the secret place of the most High shall abide under the shadow of the Almighty.

I will say of the LORD, He is my refuge and my fortress: my God; in him will I trust.

Surely he shall deliver thee from the snare of the fowler, and from the noisome pestilence.

He shall cover thee with his feathers, and under his wings shalt thou trust: his truth shall be thy shield and buckler.

Thou shalt not be afraid for the terror by night; nor for the arrow that flieth by day;

Nor for the pestilence that walketh in darkness; nor for the destruction that wasteth at noonday.

A thousand shall fall at thy side, and ten thousand at thy right hand; but it shall not come nigh thee.

Only with thine eyes shalt thou behold and see the reward of the wicked.

Because thou hast made the LORD, which is my refuge, even the most High, thy habitation;

There shall no evil befall thee, neither shall any plague come nigh thy dwelling.

For he shall give his angels charge over thee, to keep thee in all thy ways.

They shall bear thee up in their hands, lest thou dash thy foot against a stone.

Thou shalt tread upon the lion and adder: the young lion and the dragon shalt thou trample under feet.

Because he hath set his love upon me, therefore will I deliver him: I will set him on high, because he hath known my name.

He shall call upon me, and I will answer him: I will be with him in trouble; I will deliver him, and honour him.

With long life will I satisfy him, and shew him my salvation.

One thing that a Christian must understand is that God is his/her refuge. No matter what the situation is you must remember that God is in control. The scripture says in Psalm 91:11 "For he shall give his angels charge over thee, to keep thee in all thy ways." God will deliver you from the hand of the enemy. It may not always be at the time you think it will happen. It may not be in the way you expected it to come, but it will happen if you trust and believe in Him.

A Life Of Faith

Prior to my cancer diagnosis, the Lord had proven Himself to me over, and over again, even when I had not dedicated my life to Him. I can remember as far back as my college years at the University of South Florida (USF), in Tampa, Florida. I had moved off campus into an apartment with some friends. I did not personally have transportation at that time. One of my roommates had an automobile that was not in the best condition. It was the only transportation we had to get to the campus and back home. Her car would often stall. Sometimes it worked, but many times it did not.

One day my roommate, Anne, tried and tried to start the car. The engine roared like a lion and then suddenly died down to nothing. I said to her, "Just put the key in again." She said, "Janice I have tried many times."

I replied, "Then try it one more time and it will start." She followed my suggestion, and suddenly we were off to school as happy as could be.

There have been many of these faith actions throughout my life. During those years my friends often asked me, "Why don't you just go ahead and give your life to Christ?" This was because I talked about salvation all the time, but lived a life of sin.

As a young girl, I remember having a lot of faith. I learned the definition of faith at a young age, while attending Sunday School and Bible classes at church. My mother was the director of the church youth department. She often encouraged me to speak in front of the church on different occasions. In one of my youth day speeches I remember boldly giving the definition of faith in Hebrews 11:1 "Now faith is the substance of things hoped for, the evidence of things not seen."

During my school years, I remember praying for a certain grade on my tests and believing I would receive it. Many times, I knew I had not studied as I should, but I still did well. So, it was very much like me to tell my roommate to have faith that her car would start. I would tell her that God would not let us get stuck without a way to class.

God wants you to try Him at His Word. He wants you to prove Him. Sometimes we feel that we are not worthy of all this favor from God, but He is our refuge in the time of need. We must give something back to God. We must serve Him and trust Him with our lives. We must be willing to be used of Him.

Life's Challenges

My mother had always told me the story about my birth. She reminded me often that my life started with challenges. Having had so many children, I wondered how she could keep up with the history of our births and other memories. As she got older, it became a little more difficult for her to remember, but she still had an unusual memory for her age. She had told me her story so many times until I could easily remind her of the story myself.

She told me that when she was between eight and nine months pregnant with me, she became very ill. At that time, there was a virus going around that was named the *"Hong Kong Flu."* She had begun to feel very sick and was praying to God that she did not have the virus. She became more and more ill as the days went by. She was very afraid that she might go into labor.

Lo and behold, as she would often say, she did go into labor while she was very sick. I was born at that time. My grandmother was a midwife for the community and delivered me along with many other children.

Mother told me she was devastated at having to birth a child in that condition. This subject always seemed to come up when I would frequently get sick with colds, etc. During those moments, she often spoke soothing words to me in a very sympathetic tone as if she was somewhat responsible. Her thoughts were that she must have passed something on to me. I never knew if such a thing was possible, but I did know that I had a compromised immune system.

In my adult years, I found out that I was asthmatic, which could very well have contributed to my frequent colds. Throughout my life, I have had many physical challenges that are noteworthy. I had an experience in 2008 when I was suffering with uterine fibroids. I suffered for many months with frequent and/or missed menstrual cycles and heavy bleeding. I finally decided to go through a procedure called Uterine Fibroid Embolization, which shrinks the fibroids.

My faith was even tested then because some women experience a problem with a fibroid getting infected after this procedure. I happened to be one. I was threatened by many doctors in the hospital that I could not leave without a complete hysterectomy.

I was fighting the doctors because I had been in the hospital longer than expected and had a big family event coming up. I was the organizer and had all the funds in my name. I had asked my pastor to pray that I could leave the hospital. The doctors said I was severely anemic along with the other issues. I continued to tell the doctors that God would heal me even though my condition was serious.

Right about the time that I really needed to be out of the hospital to get prepared for my event, my hemoglobin count miraculously went up to normal, and the infection cleared up. I was discharged from the hospital in time to travel and without the hysterectomy. I almost literally walked out of the hospital into the charter bus for my family trip. Many may have thought it was unwise, but this is the level of faith I have always had.

I was no stranger in seeing God come through. I know first-hand that He will rescue His people. I had tried Him many times and found Him to be true. This new situation with cancer; however, was a horse of a different color. But I continued to tell myself that God would rescue me indeed!

Soldier's Creed

I have always wanted to be an example of a good Christian. This is something that is very important to me. When a person enlists in the U.S. Army, he/she is required to go through basic training. Upon enlistment, one is encouraged to adhere to a certain standard of living. At the end of the basic training a soldier is expected to recite the Soldier's Creed. This creed includes statements such as:

"I will always place the mission first."
"I will never accept defeat."
"I will never quit."

As soldiers of Christ, we are in the Army of the Lord. We are Ambassadors for Christ; however, many of us fail to realize that we must also adhere to standards and creeds set forth in the Word of God. As a Christian soldier, we too must place the mission first. Our mission is to win others to Christ and to represent Him well. We are in the world, but not of the world.

Therefore, we must not forget that we are to be an example for others. Like the Army soldier, we must never accept defeat. We must never quit. We must never give up. No matter how difficult our lives become, we must continue in the faith.

After the death and resurrection of Jesus Christ, He commanded His disciples to go and share the gospel to every nation. This is considered the Great Commission, referred to in Matthew 28:19-20.

Go ye therefore, and teach all nations, baptizing them in the name of the Father, and of the Son, and of the Holy Ghost:
Teaching them to observe all things whatsoever I have commanded you: and, lo, I am with you always, even unto the end of the world. Amen.

To fulfill this commission, you must be both a person who is standing for God, and your life must be a living testament. Therefore, when you go through trials and tribulations you must demonstrate to others that God cannot fail. No matter how difficult this task may seem when you are going through, it is possible because of the help and strength of the Lord.

Don't Give Up!

Maintaining a standard of Christian living not only helps us to witness to others about the love and healing powers of Jesus Christ, but it inspires them to not give up when they too are facing a crisis or difficult situation.

Giving up does not seem to be in my makeup. There was another time in 2010, when I suffered from what my pulmonologist diagnosed as a severe asthma attack. I remember going to work that day feeling horrible. I was not sure at all if I was in one of my asthmatic states or not.

I remember calling my doctor to ask if I could come in as an emergency appointment. He allowed me to come, and I drove myself to his office in a very bad condition. Once I reached his office, my breathing was very bad. The breathing treatments had little effect. The doctor ordered his staff to rush me across the parking lot to the hospital in a wheelchair. I was rushed into the ER and began receiving treatments immediately.

I have an issue that seems to be genetic where my veins are small and difficult to find. The medical staff had a difficult time placing an IV in my arm, as usual. I remember that another phlebotomist was called in to try the IV, after others had failed. It was taking a long time despite me being in the middle of an asthma attack. However, I was able to talk and contact my nieces who had just traveled with me back from central Florida the day before.

After some time had passed I felt breath leaving my body. They had just placed the IV in my arm. Just in the nick of time, medicine was administered through the IV to start my breathing again. My friends, Zetta and Tony, had arrived at the ER. I had called them as they happened to be near the hospital. The doctors rushed in and ordered them to leave the room. After it was all over, my friends told me how frightening this was for them.

Emergency room doctors declared that my heart stopped, and that I had Congestive Heart Failure even though my pulmonologist declared that I had an asthma attack, which was in contrast with the hospital doctors' findings. For the next few days doctors did every possible test on my heart and found that each test result was negative, and nothing was wrong with my heart. Praise God! Yes, all tests were negative.

Then I was told that I had blood clots in my lungs, and would have to be put on Coumadin for six months. After a scan of my lungs, I was then told that the spots that they saw were really dye from the test that I had taken and not blood clots. Afterwards, my legs were scanned to see if I was prone to having blood clots, which was also negative. As you can see, everything that I was told did not pan out because I serve a great God who has the last say regarding my life.

The night after this terrible asthma experience in the hospital, I had a horrible dream. In the dream, I was jumping on the graves of my twin brothers who both passed away in 2002 and 2007, respectively. I did not know the significance of this dream, but I believed that it was Satan trying to put fear of death in me. I had difficulty going to sleep after that. I had to rebuke fear, for I knew then and now that fear is not of God.

My pulmonology team still insisted that I had an asthma attack. Nevertheless, I was referred to a cardiologist for follow-up. Years later there has never been a major issue found with my heart, etc. This is just one of the many testimonies that I have of the goodness of God in my life. I always testify to my doctors and everyone else about God's goodness.

Even though I had experienced these different challenges in the past, in my mind, cancer was the real giant that I had to now face!

Giants In Our Lives

Giants! Many do not realize that there are things that occur in our lives that can be considered giants. Giants come in many forms. A giant in your life can be anything that is hindering you from achieving your goal, or trying to stop you from fulfilling the plan of God for your life.

Your giant can be a financial burden, job, ministry, sickness or many other things. To defeat that giant, it takes *prayer, strength* and *determination.* It takes a vision and a desire to fulfill your purpose. Giants *do* fall, but you must be willing to go into battle with the Lord on your side.

There is a familiar story in the Bible in 1st Samuel 17th chapter regarding a giant called Goliath. In this story, Goliath who was a Philistine, came out every morning and evening, and threatened the Israelites who were all very afraid of him.

As the story goes, David had brothers who went with King Saul to the battle every day. However, David who was the youngest son tended to his father's sheep. Then one-day David's father Jesse, sent him to take food to the captain of the army, and to check on his brothers. David had no idea what this act would lead to.

David was talking to his brothers when Goliath came out to make the normal threats that he did each day. All the other men ran in fear of this giant. However, David wanted to know more about him, and why he dared to defy the armies of God. At that time, it entered David's heart to do something about the giant.

No one really believed he could do anything about it. After all, David was only a little shepherd boy to them. David began to explain to King Saul how he slew a lion and a bear that had come against his lambs. He may have sounded convincing, but it took time for Saul to really believe him. Nevertheless, Saul decided to try David at his word.

You must also try God at His Word. If He says you can do something, then it can be done. If Jesus says by His stripes you are healed, you must believe that. Let's look at the remaining story of David and Goliath, in the scriptures.

1st Samuel 17: 38-52

And Saul armed David with his armour, and he put an helmet of brass upon his head; also he armed him with a coat of mail.

And David girded his sword upon his armour, and he assayed to go; for he had not proved it. And David said unto Saul, I cannot go with these; for I have not proved them. And David put them off him.

And he took his staff in his hand, and chose him five smooth stones out of the brook, and put them in a shepherd's bag which he had, even in a scrip; and his sling was in his hand: and he drew near to the Philistine.

And the Philistine came on and drew near unto David; and the man that bare the shield went before him.

And when the Philistine looked about, and saw David, he disdained him: for he was but a youth, and ruddy, and of a fair countenance.

And the Philistine said unto David, Am I a dog, that thou comest to me with staves? And the Philistine cursed David by his gods.

And the Philistine said to David, Come to me, and I will give thy flesh unto the fowls of the air, and to the beasts of the field. Then said David to the Philistine, Thou comest to me with a sword, and with a spear, and with a shield: but I come to thee in the name of the LORD of hosts, the God of the armies of Israel, whom thou hast defied.

This day will the LORD deliver thee into mine hand; and I will smite thee, and take thine head from thee; and I will give the carcases of the host of the Philistines this day unto the fowls of the air, and to the wild beasts of the earth; that all the earth may know that there is a God in Israel.

And all this assembly shall know that the LORD saveth not with sword and spear: for the battle is the LORD's, and he will give you into our hands.

And it came to pass, when the Philistine arose, and came, and drew nigh to meet David, that David hastened, and ran toward the army to meet the Philistine.

And David put his hand in his bag, and took thence a stone, and slang it, and smote the Philistine in his forehead, that the stone sunk into his forehead; and he fell upon his face to the earth.

So David prevailed over the Philistine with a sling and with a stone, and smote the Philistine, and slew him; but there was no sword in the hand of David.

Therefore David ran, and stood upon the Philistine, and took his sword, and drew it out of the sheath thereof, and slew him, and cut off his head therewith. And when the Philistines saw their champion was dead, they fled.

And the men of Israel and of Judah arose, and shouted, and pursued the Philistines, until thou come to the valley, and to the gates of Ekron. And the wounded of the Philistines fell down by the way to Shaaraim, even unto Gath, and unto Ekron.

We must get rid of the fear. It may not be easy, but it must be done. I too had to find strength to fight the enemy just as David did. My enemy was cancer.

3

The Furnace of Affliction

Throughout the Bible, there are many scriptures and accounts of prophets, apostles and others who went through affliction. Their stories were written to encourage us to always continuously bless God. During times of affliction, we must lift our voices in praise to Him regardless of who may be around us. God holds our lives in His hand, and won't allow us to be moved from the place He has called us to be. King David faced many afflictions, and in the book of Psalm he demonstrated how to bless the name of the Lord despite of what he was going through. Here is one scripture that displays that frame of mind:

Psalm 66:8-12.
O bless our God, ye people, and make the voice of his praise to be heard:
Which holdeth our soul in life, and suffereth not our feet to be moved.
For thou, O God, hast proved us: thou hast tried us, as silver is tried.
Thou broughtest us into the net; thou laidst affliction upon our loins.

Thou hast caused men to ride over our heads; we went through fire and through water: but thou broughtest us out into a wealthy place.

Testing

If we intend to be in a wealthy place, we must be tested. As a popular phrase, says "No test, no testimony." We will never fully understand why God allows us to go through certain situations. God demonstrates His love for us in the furnace of affliction.

Silver, just like gold, must also be refined. Silver is the lightest of the precious metals. A silversmith holds the silver in the middle of the fire, so it can be affected by the hottest flames. He also pays close attention to the silver while it is being heated up because if he takes his eyes off the silver—there is a chance it can be destroyed.

God allows us to go in the fire to rid of all impurities in our lives. For this reason, God keeps a close eye on us when we are in the furnace of affliction and won't allow the Devil to destroy us. Through it all, we must also keep our eyes on God and believe what it says in this scripture:

Isaiah 48:10
Behold, I have refined thee, but not with silver; I have chosen thee in the furnace of affliction.

God can use anything and anybody while in the furnace of affliction even though each of our furnaces may be different. For example, I know people who have suffered greatly in the area of employment, finding it difficult to obtain a job and/or maintaining one. Another example is people who have had a very difficult time in maintaining good relationships and go from one relationship to another. Then there are people who struggle with their personal finances more than others.

In my life, I have indeed encountered various struggles, specifically illnesses. However, there are other areas as described above in which I have not had to deal with as much. One personal example is with employment. I can proudly say that since I graduated from college and obtained my first job, I have never been unemployed for any reason in my adult life.

I attribute this to the grace of God. It's not that I couldn't have lost a job, for I am not perfect. Like others, on my jobs I have made some mistakes, and have had difficulties with certain people. I have arrived late on a job, been out ill or may have done other things that could have caused me to be unemployed. However, by the grace of God, I was employed for over 35 years. My point is that all of us have different afflictions, but we must not allow these situations to break us.

It is difficult for many to understand why a faithful Christian goes through losses. One thing that we must understand is that we must praise God through the situations we encounter in life. We must bless God amid the circumstances, as this scripture tells us:

Psalm 92: 1-2
It is a good thing to give thanks unto the LORD, and to sing praises unto thy name, O Most High:
To shew forth thy lovingkindness in the morning, and thy faithfulness every night.

Praising God confuses the enemy of our soul. No matter how we feel, and no matter what it looks like, we must praise God for His goodness. If we learn this lesson, though we will go through the fire, and through the water, we will come through as pure gold.

Isaiah 43:2
When thou passest through the waters, I will be with thee; and through the rivers, they shall not overflow thee: when thou walkest

through the fire, thou shalt not be burned; neither shall the flame kindle upon thee.

Moving On

It would be nice if we could pick our tests and our trials. In my case, I didn't know a harder trial to face than a cancer diagnosis. In January of 2012, after leaving the hospital where I received my cancer diagnosis, I felt as if I was walking around with a brick on my shoulders. Yes, my faith told me to believe that this was all a mistake, to keep loving God anyway, and trusting Him with all my heart.

My mind was telling me that the doctor's diagnosis was most likely correct, but a host of questions were dancing around in my head. Some of my thoughts were "What if I really do have cancer?" Will I be like the young track star that I saw on television in the hospital room the morning I received the diagnosis?" "Will I make it through enough to win a race, as she did with her right leg still intact?" My mind was flooded with what ifs!!!!

Yes, the days after I left the hospital were filled with thoughts of the journey I was about to embark on. I told a few friends and family members to be praying and standing in faith with me. I told them I knew this was going to turn out to be a misdiagnosis and that I was not worried just concerned. However, in my mind the what ifs kept ringing out.

I prayed like never. I called on God and asked Him to let this all be a dream. I asked God to let the pain go away. The pain medication could temporarily stop the pain, but it could not stop the wondering mind.

The time was getting closer and closer for me to go to a scheduled appointment at the University of Miami Hospital to get a confirmation of the cancer diagnosis. Little did I know that I had just begun my time in the furnace, and I was about to really go further.

Final Diagnosis

The days since my cancer diagnosis seemed to drag on then it was finally time. Since I lived in Miami away from most of my family members who mainly live in central Florida, I needed to depend on others. I had one sister, Peggy, in South Florida, but due to distance I did not solicit her to accompany me to my initial appointment. My friend, Veronica, drove me to the hospital, dropped me off then left immediately because she needed to go to her job to take care of some things. She promised to return as soon as possible.

I should have felt alone after she left, but there were too many things already crowded in my mind. I walked into the doctor's office and signed in to see the referred physician, Dr. Harry Thomas Temple, Oncology Orthopedic Surgeon. He and two additional doctors whom I did not expect to see, were in the room with us.

Dr. Temple introduced himself and the other doctors. I learned that one of them would later be my radiation doctor. By the time they started talking, my friend Veronica returned, and I was relieved that I did not have to hear the news alone after all.

Dr. Temple began to explain that he and his team of doctors had reviewed my records from the previous hospital. He said after reviewing the MRI results and the other records, he and his staff concurred with the diagnosis of a soft tissue sarcoma tumor in my right ham string area. He explained that soft tissue sarcoma tumors may develop in any tissue that connects, supports or surrounds other structures and organs in the body.

Some examples of where soft tissue tumors can develop are muscles, fascia (the tough membrane that surrounds muscles), tendons, fat, blood vessels, nerves and synovial tissues (Connective tissue that makes up the membranes surrounding joints).

As he was talking, I felt as if I was having an out-of-body experience. I asked Veronica to please listen carefully as I could not really focus on what was being said. I remember blurting out, "I know God has this under control." The doctors gave me a sympathetic look as if they had heard this wishful thinking many times before.

My mind floated in and out of the conversation, and from that point on I only heard bits and pieces of the information. I was devastated. All I could think was*"How could this be?"* Finally, I heard Dr. Temple say, "Ms. Harris we can do one last thing to confirm the diagnosis. We can do a biopsy that will be completed in about fifteen minutes, and give you the results before you leave this office."

That seemed like the longest fifteen minutes of my life. I squirmed nervously in my seat as we waited. Waiting is never easy, especially when it could possibly be bad news. Just as he said, the doctors returned to the room in about fifteen minutes. The announcement was made loud and clear. "Ms. Harris, we are 100% sure that your tumor is cancerous and is grade 3," said Dr. Temple. I was told this meant that the tumor was growing very aggressively. I knew it had to be aggressive since the tumor had grown very large in the short period from early December to now mid-January.

So, now it was final to me that my journey had begun! Dr. Temple explained that there are about 50 types of Sarcoma cancer. My medical records show that I was diagnosed with a Pleomorphic Fibroblastic/Myofibroblastic Sarcoma. He stated that I would need to be treated with radiation first. Then he explained that the doctor who was to complete the radiation would be going on a scheduled vacation for two weeks. They would begin my treatments when he returned. I was not sure how I felt about this news. Besides, I wondered how could they wait so long when the tumor was growing aggressively. I had to trust in their expertise. I was somewhat relieved that I had some more time to process this awful and shocking news.

After I had been given all the pertinent information, my friend and I left the doctor's office. Needless to say, it was a long drive home.

The Cancer Journey Begins

As I rode home from the doctor's office I was very silent and in complete disbelief. I could not even digest what had just happened. My head was spinning, and I felt lightheaded. Something inside of me was still believing that it could be a mistake, but I knew what I had to do. I knew I had to solicit prayers from every person who I believed knew the words of prayer.

I remembered the scripture – James 5:16 that says, "The effectual fervent prayer of a righteous man availeth much." I knew I had to call on the Lord more than ever before. I knew I had to pray harder than I had ever prayed in my life. I knew I had to be strong and diligent in my expectations that God *could and would* turn this situation around.

Waiting for two weeks was the hardest thing I had ever done. Meanwhile, I did solicit the prayers of many. My pastor, Reverend Vickers, prayed and assured me that I could go through this fire that had been ignited and would change my life forever. My family members were also devastated when I relayed the news to them. Again, I knew my family had been through so much. Too much! I didn't want to see them go through this again at all, especially not so soon.

Those who knew my diagnosis encouraged me. Many of them told me it would be alright. Did I really believe it? I began to read scriptures of healing and settled in my mind and heart that I would have to make it through this, but I had no clue as to how I would do it. *But God did!*

My sister Peggy, was to become my companion through what seemed like the start of a forest fire. A fire can be very destructive, or it can be extremely helpful. To start a fire, it takes a chemical reaction typically between oxygen and fuel. With a combination of many things, a fire can become extremely hot. If it is not tended to properly it can burn out of control. A forest fire or a wild fire happens when uncontrolled blazes are fueled by different elements such as weather, wind, dry underbrush, etc. It is said that wildfires can burn acres of land and consume everything in their path within a few minutes.

Also, a wildfire moves at speeds of up to 14 miles an hour, consuming everything in its pathway. I felt like this fire that had begun in my life had been set so fast and uncontrollable that I barely had time for my mind to catch up with the actions. The fire seemed to be consuming every part of my life. Yet, I knew I had to somehow get the strength, the faith, and the wherewithal to combat this wildfire and slow it down—even stop it before it destroyed my life.

Peggy lived about 30 minutes from my home, and since she and her husband are both retired I knew I had to depend on them to help me through this terrible time in my life. Friends were not able to help as much due to their jobs and busy lives, but I knew I could benefit from their prayers and well-wishes. At difficult times in your life, you need cheerleaders. You need people who can inspire you not to give up.

The Shadow Of Death

One of the most memorable moments for me was when I had a telephone conversation with a long-time friend and past church member who lives in Bradenton, Florida. Reverend Dr. Carolyn McKinnon, a prophetic voice in my life, spoke some words to me that took me a long way. She said, "Janice you will go through a lot, but just remember what the Word of God says in **Psalm 23:4.**"

Yea, though I walk through the valley of the shadow of death, I will fear no evil: for thou art with me; thy rod and thy staff they comfort me.

She told me to focus on the word *"shadow."* She said, "What you will go through will seem like death, but it is just a *"shadow"* and God will be with you." I clung to those words throughout my trial like a baby clinging to its mother for life and support.

Beginning The Process

During my first visit with the doctors at UMHC, it had been explained that the type of sarcoma cancer that I had would need radiation treatments then chemotherapy. However, my secondary visit had revealed that due to the aggressiveness of the tumor, I would need to start with chemo. I was not happy about this news because after all, I had waited for several weeks.

I was given an appointment at the Sylvester Comprehensive Cancer Center in Miami, which is a part of UMHC. My appointment was with Dr. Jonathan Trent, Oncologist, who would oversee my chemo. During my first visit with him, he said I would need to complete five sessions of chemo, five days each. During that visit, I felt that God had placed me in good hands.

I learned that Dr. Trent had recently come on board at this center. He had previously been on staff at M.D. Anderson in Houston, Texas. Dr. Trent and his Physician's Assistant Elizabeth, were very kind and encouraging. He scheduled me to report for my first chemo treatment.

It was explained that due to my situation, it would be best for me to be hospitalized for my chemo sessions. He informed me that after each session I would be discharged for a two-week break before returning. This arrangement would later prove to be a good decision.

Since my diagnosis, I had enveloped myself in prayer and supplication. I felt very confident that I could be an overcomer. I told myself this repeatedly. No matter how many times I told myself that I could go through this fire, my flesh would try to tell me differently. Of course, the enemy of your soul (the Devil) will tell you that you cannot make it. In my case, I could not afford to believe it.

Seeds Of Doubt

When I went for an appointment with Dr. Trent, I was sitting outside the building waiting for my transportation. A very kind woman sat next to me.

She was dressed well and looked well. I had no reason to believe that she was a cancer patient until she initiated a conversation with me.

I began to tell her my reason for being there. She in turn told me a portion of her story. She said she was there for her last appointment after completing chemo, and that she was a survivor. I asked her about hair loss because she seemed to be wearing her natural hair, and it looked very healthy. She explained to me that she had not really lost her hair during the process. I was amazed. It was such a pleasant and promising conversation.

After I arrived home from my appointment, you would think that I would have felt better about the journey that I was about to embark on, but this was not the case. I had begun to feel very down. The Devil had placed seeds of doubt in my mind. This would be the first and only time in my cancer journey that I felt almost hopeless.

I told myself that I would not do any chemo or radiation treatments. I thought, after all, "Why would God allow this to happen to me?" I said in my mind that if God had allowed me to have cancer then undoubtedly it was meant for my life to come to an end.

I told myself that I was going to inform everyone of my decision and what led to it. I really could not explain this sudden feeling. I picked up my phone and called Reverend Vickers. I began to tell him how I was feeling. Obviously, he was not willing to join in my pity party, and he helped to set my mind in order. By the time our conversation ended, I was again ready to go through this fire that had been set in my life.

Therefore, in February of 2012, my sister and I reported to Sylvester Comprehensive Cancer Center to begin my treatment. I was immediately impressed with the hospital and the staff. This was the start of a long journey with this very kind doctor who became an integral part of my cancer process.

Even though I felt very confident with the hospital staff nothing could really and truly calm my nerves except my faith in the Lord God almighty.

4

Oh Lord, I Am But Clay

Isaiah 64:8
"But now, O LORD, thou art our father; we are the clay, and thou our potter; and we all are the work of thy hand."

E ver since I gave my life to the Lord at the age of twenty-four, I have tried to live my life as the Lord would have me to. However, as with all of us, I have made mistakes. I have sinned and come short. I have stumbled, and even fallen at times. Surely, the Lord has kept me.

As you walk this Christian journey, you will need reminders along the way that you are but clay. You must remember that in your sin and faults God is your father, and only He can make you what you ought to be. You must also remember that only God is in complete control to mold and shape us. He alone knows our beginning, our end, how we think of ourselves, but more importantly it matters what God thinks of us.

As I checked into the cancer center in February, I evaluated all that I had done and had not done for the Lord. I was mindful that the Bible assures us God will not forget our labor of love. I believed God would remember all the good things that I had done for people, and the person that I had become. Somehow, I felt that although I was not perfect, I had lived my life in such a way — that if I called on the Lord, He would answer me.

So, I went into the cancer center with confidence that God was not through with me yet. I knew that He still had something for me to do, and had someone that I needed to minister to. The biggest task at hand was ministering to myself. I had to believe that God could and would bring me to an expected end, and that I would live. Just as the three Hebrew men were in the fire and came out without even their clothes smelling like smoke, I had to believe that I would come out of this situation in a condition that would be an encouragement to someone else with cancer or any other dreadful disease. Thus, my chemo treatments started, and I yielded myself to the Lord to take me through the journey.

The Fire Heats Up

As the nurses connected the IVs, I listened as they all complained that my oncologist did things different from all the other doctors. They whispered that he was the new kid on the block and that he did not use the ports that all the doctors were using to administer treatments. Instead, Dr. Trent, used the PICC line (Peripherally Inserted Central Catheter) for his patients, which is a long, thin, hollow tube that a doctor or nurse puts into a vein above the bend of the elbow. It is used to provide IV access to administer long-time medications. It can usually stay in place until the treatment is over.

I really didn't know the difference, but I later found out my PICC lines continuously had to be removed because they had gotten infected. The one thing I overheard many times from all the nursing staff was that even though my doctor was different, all his patients seemed to be doing well, and the mixture of chemo medications he prescribed was shrinking his patients' tumors. They said his chemo mixtures were not like the other doctors, and they were having difficulties learning how to hang the IV bags, etc. I felt a sense of trust and believed that Dr. Trent was doing what was best for me.

The five days of my first chemo session went better than I thought it would, even though I was extremely weak and exhausted. I slept sometimes through an entire day and would wake up and ask what day it was. I did not experience some of the symptoms such as vomiting as my roommates did. I do remember that I could not stand to eat or smell chicken at all. My appetite was very poor, and I struggled in many ways. Overall, I felt I was doing okay — because to put it simply, I was alive! Since UMHC/Sylvester Cancer Center is a teaching hospital, I was visited every day by a team of doctors evaluating me and asking a series of questions. I felt like the only sarcoma case in the world.

Prior to my hospitalization, a family friend, Reverend Jones from my hometown, had sent me a small book with healing scriptures. Each night whenever I could stay awake I read the scriptures out loud to myself. Also, my co-worker and friend Maria, had given me a couple of CDs with praise music. Those items became my constant companions throughout my time of treatment.

After the first five days were over, my hopes were shattered when I was told that I could not go home as scheduled. Doctors told me it was because I had a high fever in the tumor. I did not understand this because I had been experiencing this fever from the time the tumor first developed.

Every few days I was told by the doctors and nurses that they had to take a culture from my tumor and study it to make sure I did not have an infection. Anyone who touched my thigh could feel that it was extremely hot. I was disappointed, but I accepted that it was doctor's orders. I knew the doctors had my best interest in mind.

Even though I slept heavily every day, I looked forward to my family visiting me. There is nothing like looking up and seeing faces of people who you truly love. I knew it was very hard for them to see me in that condition; nevertheless, they braved the storm.

Each day came and went, and I was still told I could not go home. There were MRIs, tests and constant checks by the nursing staff. I was so disappointed as I felt I needed to see the light of day. One never knows how valuable it is just to step outside in the daylight until one is not able to do so.

I had roommates who were placed in the bed by the window. For some reason, I never complained. My roommates, except for one, were not very pleasant. I had one roommate who decided that she would just be miserable. She seemed to be determined to make everyone else around her as miserable as she was.

She decided to pick a fight with me. It seemed she was not happy with the way the nurses interacted with me. There was usually laughter and cheerfulness surrounding me with the nurses and my family members. This particular roommate fought with everyone and threatened the doctors to leave the hospital without completing her treatment. At a crucial time, such as this, a patient needs peace and not someone who wants to make everyone else miserable. I made up my mind to just pray for her, and I constantly asked the Lord to help her. I understood that many people become bitter when their lives are threatened by an ugly disease such as cancer. However, I refused to have a bitter disposition.

As I said, the nurses and staff seemed to enjoy coming to my room. I even let one of the nurses listen to one of the CDs. I was in constant and extreme pain. I could never sleep on my right side. As a matter of fact, I had not slept on my right side since the ordeal began. Since I am one who has always slept on my side, (never ever on my back or stomach) sleeping was very difficult unless I was medicated.

I longed for the opportunity to go home, but it seemed as if the time would never come. Through it all, I maintained a positive attitude even while suffering. I understood that this was what the Lord required of me. I knew I needed to allow God to mold and shape me even in my horrible condition.

Weeks went by, and I had to endure the constant news that I was not well enough to go home. Many times, I had to remember that I was only clay. I had to remember that I needed God to have His own way in my life. I reached out in my own way to each new roommate to comfort them spiritually even though I too was suffering. I just wanted God to have His way in my life! I wanted to live so I could help someone else.

Have Thine All Way Lord!

It was said that in 1907, a woman named Adelaide A. Pollard, believed God wanted her in Africa as a missionary, but she was unable to raise funds to go. In an uncertain state of mind, she attended a prayer meeting, where she heard an elderly woman pray, "It's all right, Lord. It doesn't matter what You bring into our lives just have your own way with us." At home that night, much encouraged, she wrote the hymn – "Have Thine Own Way Lord."

Have Thine own way, Lord! Have Thine own way!
Thou art the Potter, I am the clay. Mold me and make me
after Thy will, While I am waiting, yielded and still.
Have Thine own way, Lord! Have Thine own way!
Search me and try me, Master, today!
Whiter than snow, Lord, wash me just now,
As in Thy presence humbly I bow.
Have Thine own way, Lord! Have Thine own way!
Wounded and weary, help me, I pray!
Power, all power, surely is Thine!
Touch me and heal me, Savior divine.
Have Thine own way, Lord! Have Thine own way!
Hold o'er my being absolute sway! Fill with Thy Spirit
'till all shall see Christ only, always, living in me.

I needed God to have His way in my life. I had yielded myself to the Lord. Though I was licensed as a minister in 1998, I was a person who really did not care very much about titles. However, I had been working in ministry for many years and I knew there was more that the Lord wanted out of my life.

I had always known that I needed God to continue to mold and shape me after His will. Now, I understood that even more. I understood that life could have many surprises. I had learned that life could bring changes and challenges that could shake you to the very core. Having Jesus Christ in our lives is an assurance that, if we allow Him, He can take us through the storms.

When you ask the Lord to have His way in your life, it means that you must step out of the way. God's ways and His thoughts are higher than yours. You must not confuse what you think or feel, with God's way and His will for your life. I wanted to believe very badly that God was allowing my suffering because He was preparing me for greater things. I knew that this was an entirely new chapter in the book of my life. I also knew that only God knew the end, and I had to trust Him to reveal it in due time.

Jeremiah 18:1-6

The word which came to Jeremiah from the LORD, saying,
Arise, and go down to the potter's house, and there I will cause thee to hear my words.
Then I went down to the potter's house, and, behold, he wrought a work on the wheels.
And the vessel that he made of clay was marred in the hand of the potter: So he made it again another vessel, as seemed good to the potter to make it.
Then the word of the LORD came to me, saying,
O house of Israel, cannot I do with you as this potter? saith the LORD. Behold, as the clay is in the potter's hand, so are ye in mine hand, O house of Israel.

The Potter

Yes, I was in the Potter's hand. I knew I needed Him to keep not only working on me, but to make me whole. I needed a miracle in my life. For the potter to do his work, you must be yielded and still. You must allow him to work in his own time.

Clay may be useless to most people. However, a potter sees a vision and knows that much can be done with something that others may just trample on. This is how God sees us. We are somebody to Him.

The process of a potter has not changed very much from the days of Jeremiah. A lump of clay is still a lump of clay that must be kneaded, pounded, twisted and shaped for it to be ready for use. Just as gold, silver, and other valuable products, impurities must be removed from the clay then taken to the next process which is the wheel.

If the clay is not perfect at the time the potter needs to continue the process, he does not just throw the lump of clay away, but He takes the same lump and reshapes it until it fits the requirements needed to complete the next step of the process. The potter's wheel is used to help smooth and refine the clay. Even after the potter spins the clay on the wheel, he/she may still need to try to remove any impurities that may have slipped in. The potter does not give up, but continues the process of the centering, to perfect the clay into a beautiful vessel.

There are quite a few steps left after the potter's wheel, but he/she must be determined to see it through to the end. The potter starts out with a vision of what he/she wants it to look like in the end. To God, we are but clay. He will continue to work in us, and through us until He makes us what we need to be. There are many ways for Him to accomplish this as He has a plan for all of us. We must be willing to let Him take us through the process, including the good and the bad.

Praise Your Way Through

Colossians 3:16
Let the word of Christ dwell in you richly in all wisdom; teaching and admonishing one another in psalms and hymns and spiritual songs, singing with grace in your hearts to the Lord.

Psalm 100:4
Enter into his gates with thanksgiving, and into his courts with praise: be thankful unto him, and bless his name.

Throughout the Bible, we see that God requires us to praise Him. We are told that "He inhabits the praises of His people." Praise is an important part of a Christian's walk with the Lord. During many trials in my life, I had learned this fairly well. I was by no means perfect, but after situations occurred in my life I had the tendency to pick myself up quickly with the help of the Lord. I knew while I was in this fire, (my cancer journey), I certainly had no choice but to praise my way through.

I had heard about, and seen people with hair loss after chemo treatments. I was not sure whether I had mentally prepared myself for that or not. To illustrate, during one of the visits from my sisters Peggy, Valeria, and my niece Kami, that dreadful thing happened. My sister Valeria, had traveled to Miami. It was during their visit one night that Valeria offered to wash my hair. As she was taking down my braids she learned that what looked to be a full head of hair was not really a full head of hair.

As she combed out each braid my hair literally came out in the comb. By the end of the process we had filled a plastic grocery bag with my hair. I had one strand of hair still on my head. As I looked around, my sister Peggy was crying silently to herself. She kept her head turned in hopes that I didn't notice. My niece, Kami, had a look on her face as if she was about to do the same. Valeria was standing to the back of me, so I was unable to see her face. There was a stark silence in the room. No one really knew what to say. From one minute to the next, I was bald.

I did not cry that night, nor any day afterwards, over my hair. I knew I had so much to praise God for, and He alone gave me the mind to realize that the hair was not the end for me. I knew that my hair could grow back, and it did.

Going Home

After being in the cancer center for five weeks (instead of five days) after my first session of chemo, I finally got the news that I could go home for a couple of weeks and return for my second session. What joy it was to see the light of day again! I could hardly believe that I was going home. Home to me at that time was not my place of residence, but my sister's house in Pompano Beach, Florida.

I could not return to my place of residence in Miami, as we were not sure if I would be able to care for myself. I had roommates, but they were employed, and would not be able to take care of me in the way that my sister and her husband Reverend Nathaniel, could. They were both retired and even though they were heavily involved in church activities, they had time for me.

I was still very weak from being in the hospital bed for those five weeks. However, none of that mattered to me at that time. While riding home from the hospital it seemed as if I had never seen the light of day before. The sky looked different than I had ever remembered. The clouds seemed to be more beautiful than ever. The trees looked like they were swaying to a melodious sound — with the wind softly touching every branch and leaf.

I felt like I had been given new life, a new chance, and a new beginning. I felt at that moment that I was the most blessed person on earth. I was still in pain, but the pain seemed trivial compared to the beauty I was experiencing on my ride home. Only a person who has been diagnosed with a terminal illness can understand this fully. When you have been told that something has invaded your body, and that it is life threatening, you find joy in what others take for granted.

During the time of trial, it is a wonderful thing to have someone who is willing to care for you and encourage you. I had friends and church members who inquired with my family about my well-being, but during my five weeks stay I had few visitors. I knew I had a host of people praying for me, which helped to keep me going.

My sister was not sure just how much assistance I would need while staying with her. I knew it was a concern for her. I was so grateful to God that I needed little assistance in terms of my personal care. Yet I was still very weak, and my appetite remained poor. I was still unable to smell chicken and certain other foods.

Peggy and my brother-in-law cooked my meals, etc. She made my bed and anything else she needed to do for me. I could barely get through a meal because almost all food tasted awful. I knew they could cook well, but my taste buds could not tell.

I had to be grateful for everything big or small. I knew it was only days before I would have to return to the cancer center for further treatment. I also knew I had to appreciate watching television, having conversation, and just being alive.

I was trying to get used to a bald head. My sweet niece, Angelique, in Atlanta sent me several beautiful scarves to wrap my head. I had always loved wrapping my head, so this was not a big deal to me. Well, this time it was not for fun or a bad hair day, but I needed them. There were days when I decided to just go without anything covering my head. This was called *"freedom"* to me. Even so, I never shed a tear, at least not over the loss of my hair. I was still praising my way through the storm!

A Storm

I have learned something from a natural storm. When driving through heavy rains, it is often better to continue driving than to risk stopping on the side of a road or highway. Many accidents occur with vehicles parked while trying to avoid continuing through a storm. If you keep driving, before you know it you are out of the storm. This has happened to me many times.

Also, my long-time friend, Sherry, taught me that while driving through a storm in the daytime where the visibility is very low, you can put on your sunglasses to see the road clearer. When I first heard this, I did not believe it at all. Then one day I tried it and indeed it worked.

The lines on the highway are much easier to see. The darkness of the sunglasses somehow cuts through the fog that is obstructing your view. Likewise, this is how it is when you continue to praise God in the midst of your storm. The longer you keep praising Him, the clearer you see your way through. God opens your eyes to His shining light. It is a light that gives you hope.

1 Thessalonians 5:18:
In every thing give thanks: for this is the will of God in Christ Jesus concerning you.

Deeply Rooted

To praise God and give Him thanks in every situation in your life, it is important to be rooted and grounded in the Word of God. This is not to say that a non-saved person or a babe in Christ cannot praise God in the time of trouble. In other words, the closer you are to Christ and the more experience you have in praising Him, the better your chance of survival.

It is said that there are trees that do not have a very good root system. However, when a tree such as the oak has a good root system it can stand through winds and other circumstances. The tree is strengthened rather than weakened by the elements surrounding it. In like manner, when a drought takes place, the tree's roots sink deep into the ground to find the water that is needed to nourish it.

Passing a large tree such as an oak tree, you are unable to see how deep or strong the roots are. If the roots are not strong and nourished then the tree will not stand firm, as it takes years for a tree of such to grow strong and be deeply rooted. As you can see from the example of a tree, there is a time and a season for everything under the sun. As illustrated, there is a time when the tree's roots must be strengthened and there is a time in which people with different types of storms in their lives must be able to hold out.

As a Christian, you must seek the face of God not just when trouble is in your life, but daily. You must fast and pray while you are able to do so. This is the way that you can be like that tree, strong and able to withstand all the storms in your life.

In Luke 22:31 Jesus told Simon Peter "Behold Satan hath desired to have you, that he may sift you as wheat." In the 32nd verse Jesus said, "But I have prayed for thee, that thy faith fail not: and when thou art converted, strengthen thy brethren." Jesus knows everything about you. He is standing at the right hand of God and interceding for you. He knows when you are weak, afraid, tempted, etc. He knows when you are going through the storms in your life, and He is ready and willing to help you.

I continued to be in the Potter's hands, and knew these hands were able to hold me and make me what I needed to be spiritually, physically, emotionally and mentally. He alone could make me whole. He is able!

I had to trust Him all the way.

5

Diamond In The Rough

The phrase "Diamonds are a Girl's Best Friend," was made popular in a 1949 musical. Diamonds are the most popular gemstone. Women are sometimes ecstatic when they receive a diamond, especially if it is an engagement ring.

Any research about a diamond reveals that its characteristics are its hardness and that it is unbreakable. Another attraction about a diamond is its high dispersion of light, characterized as "fire" because of the light that it gives. Who would not want to be given diamonds? I absolutely love them.

Even with all the glory associated with a diamond, it is known that when a diamond is found in a mine it is not considered beautiful. In fact, it actually looks like a glassy rock or a rock of salt. A diamond is just carbon/charcoal but in a very concentrated form. It is formed under extreme temperatures and high pressure. However, when a jeweler or expert gets the diamond, it is his/her job to clean it up, cut it, and polish it. After this process has been completed, the diamond begins to shine, and it looks beautiful to a person who is interested in purchasing it.

You, as a Christian, must go through fiery trials to become like that beautiful diamond. You must be a willing vessel and able to endure the trials that cause you to be that well-disciplined person God wants you to be.

Sometimes others may look at us as if we have little value or potential. It is then that the phrase "Diamond in the Rough" may be applicable. The Urban Dictionary defines "Diamond in the Rough" as "Someone (or something) that has hidden exceptional characteristics and/or future potential, but currently lacks the final touches that would make them (or it) truly stand out from the crowd".

The good thing about God is that He sees potential in all of us. He made us and knows us. He knows that we are flesh. He knows that sometimes we may be afraid; that sometimes we doubt our own ability to thrive, and that we may not feel sure of what we can become.

I am grateful for my parents, Lonnie and Marian, who encouraged me to be the best that I could be. Both my mother and father had previous marriages. She had four children at the time she met my father who was over twenty years older than her. Together they had twelve more children. Even though money was scarce, my father worked several jobs to make sure we were well fed and clothed. Mother was often complimented for making sure we were clean and presentable when we went to school, church and other places. There were so many times in my childhood that I wanted to do certain things, but money was just not available.

Mom exposed us to community and church activities as much as possible. She was proud to see her children achieve a college or vocational education, and/or employment of any kind. She celebrated with us for any achievement, big or small. When my dad became ill in his mid-70's, my mother had to resign from a job she had secured with the local Community Action Agency (CAA).

Unfortunately, dad passed away when I was thirteen years old. My mother continued to raise and push us to achieve. Even though she was a smart woman, she completed only a high school education. There was nothing to hang her head down about as she had been at the top of her class. She had excellent writing skills and wrote hundreds of poems and prose in her spare time.

Mom even self-published a small book in her 70's, and won quite a few poetry contests. Her writings were often read or published in church literature. Although there were people who looked down on mom for having so many children, she did not let that stop her. After I completed high school mom fulfilled her dream to provide us with better housing. While she was working, she had been turned down for financing to purchase a home. She refused to accept defeat.

She already owned the property which was passed down from my grandmother, so it was a matter of how she would get this house built. Through much prayer and planning, mom decided to build our home from ground up. Some family members were able to do basically all the work that was needed. There were certain things that had to be done with the help of outside sources.

Even though a few neighbors and friends laughed when the construction on our house would stop for months, mom still plowed through. In 1976, we moved into our new four-bedroom house, built with love.

This proved to be a lesson in my life. I knew what faith was all about. I knew that when others think you cannot achieve something, or accomplish anything, that you cannot give up. I knew when I encountered a problem I had to speak faith in that situation. You must be like the diamond –- unbreakable and willing to go through the cutting, shaping and polishing to be all that you can be.

Even though the heat was being turned up in my life, I had to believe that in the end I would shine. When others don't see your beauty and your worth, you must believe in yourself. You must believe that God has a purpose for your life. You must believe when doctors look at you and say it may be over for you, that you can live!

Psalm 139:14
I will praise thee; for I am fearfully and wonderfully made: marvellous are thy works; and that my soul knoweth right well.

Prayer

Dear God, help us to realize our worth. Help us to believe that you are our strong tower. Give us the faith to withstand in the time of trouble, and to know that we can come out of our situations stronger and mightier because of you. You know what is in us. You know what we need. Lord, open our eyes to see that the enemy comes to steal, kill and destroy. Help us to understand that we can make it with the Lord on our side. Help us to believe in your Word.

6

God Is In Your Struggles

When you are struggling to survive, it is easy to forget that God is there. It is during this time a transformation needs to take place. For example, if you are suffering from a terminal illness such as I was, not only do you need a transformation (a major change in appearance or form) in your body, but also in your mind.

Accepting the Lord as our Savior, we are transformed to keep our minds stayed on Jesus, to live a righteous and holy life and to handle struggles. Having a mind like Christ is a key to Christian living and survival. There must be a change in us, and we must love God with all our hearts, mind and soul.

You must get rid of the old man, which is the way you thought and acted in the past before you came to know the Lord. Our actions must match up to our renewed mind.

This is very important when you are going through trials and tribulations. If your mind is transformed, it helps you to believe that the same Jesus who touched you in so many ways and washed you from your sin, is the same one who can touch your body and make you whole. The Word of God assures us that we were healed by the stripes that Jesus took on His body. He was wounded for our transgressions.

Being transformed though, you're not exempt from struggles and afflictions; as you will go through some dark times in your life. No matter how dark it gets, there is always light at the end of the tunnel. Trusting God is a key to your survival.

A butterfly does not start out beautiful. Instead it must go through a process of struggles, darkness, and the appropriate stages before becoming a caterpillar. Once the stages are completed, it becomes the butterfly that is then admired by many. While you are going through turmoil in your life, it may look like the process will never be completed. It may look like your situation may never end. No matter how hard you pray and call on God, it may seem that there is no help available. However, you must hold on and go through the struggle. Your wings may not be strong in the beginning, but if you keep going you will find the strength to fly high just as the butterfly.

Trouble Doesn't Last Always

Job 14:1
Man that is born of a woman is of few days and full of trouble.

The Bible clearly lets us know that each of us will face trouble in our lives. In other words, none of us are immune to things going wrong in our lives. When I first gave my life to the Lord, I honestly thought I had now alleviated big problems in my life. I am not sure where I got that idea from because that is certainly not in the Word of God.

In the story of Job, we find that Job was not an evil and sinful man. However, trouble came upon him. It may be difficult for us to understand why a person who is living upright before the Lord would find him/herself in a battle for his/her life.

Job 1: 1

There was a man in the land of Uz, whose name was Job; and that man was perfect and upright, and one that feared God, and eschewed evil.

As the story goes on, God asks Satan had he considered Job.

Job 1:8

The LORD said unto Satan, Hast thou considered my servant Job, that there is none like him in the earth, a perfect and an upright man, one that feareth God, and escheweth evil?

So, one may wonder why did God allow a righteous and faithful man such as Job to be taken through so much trouble and sickness. Job lost all that he had, including his children. There was a great ending to the story as everything was restored to Job even more than he had before. The inspiration in this story is that trouble does not last always for those of us who are serving the Lord.

The question is what must it have felt like to Job even when his friends came to him and did not really offer him comfort. Oftentimes, when a Christian is going through a sickness or other trouble, he/she will find out who his/her real friends are. As a case in point, if you are sick there may be someone who judges you as to what you have done wrong. Because of this many people do not bother to come around when a person is sick, especially if he/she is shut in or hospitalized, which is even worse. It often leads to the ill person feeling lonely and discarded by those whom they love or thought loved them.

It is very important that everyone has a personal relationship with God because in times of trouble, you need a Savior. You need someone that you can call on and who will be there regardless of what is going on in your life. People may put you down, forget about you, judge you and doubt you. Jesus will always be there.

There are so many more examples in the Bible of people who loved God yet experienced trouble. Another story that easily comes to my mind is the story of Ruth. In Ruth 1st chapter, we find that there was a famine in Bethlehem in Judah. So, a man named Elimelech, moved to the country of Moab with his wife Naomi, and their two sons. While there, Naomi's husband died then about ten years later, her two sons died.

The story goes on to say that after finding out the famine was over, Naomi decided to go back to her home in Bethlehem in Judah. Her two daughters-in-laws, Ruth and Orpah, set out to go with her, but only Ruth stayed on the journey and refused to go back to Moab as instructed by Naomi. Upon arriving back to her hometown, Ruth was blessed with work and later a marriage to Boaz.

Even though there was a great ending for Naomi and Ruth, what must people have been saying about Naomi? You can imagine that there was talk all around town with people wondering what in the world must be going on with her. I am sure some were asking the question, "What did Naomi do so wrong to lose her husband and both of her sons?" Some theologians try to answer that question as to what Ruth and her husband had done wrong such as possibly having moved out of God's will to another place.

Trouble does not last always. If we serve the lord with all our hearts, minds and souls it will bring us to a good end. Yes, it is true that some Christians die from illness. Many of them are renowned leaders including prophets, pastors, and the like. However, if they were living righteously before the Lord, it is indeed a good end because Heaven is their reward.

These are mysteries that we will never understand. All the prophets and disciples of Christ lost their lives in ways in which we may not understand. We must place our complete trust in God that He is Omnipotent (Having unlimited power; able to do anything), and He is Omniscient

(Knowing everything). God is also Omnipresent (Everywhere). He alone knows the plan for our lives.

God has a purpose and destiny for all of us. Perhaps those who have died as a result of illness had fulfilled their purpose on earth. The late Dr. Myles Munroe often said that we should "die empty." He explained that the cemetery is the wealthiest place on earth. He gave examples how the cemetery is full of books that were never written, music never heard, paintings never seen, poetry never read, etc. He said we should die with nothing else left to do because we poured out all our dreams, etc. He said, *"Don't die old, but die empty."*

So, in other words we all have a purpose. I knew no matter how tough the journey was I must trust the Lord that my trouble would not last always.

Trouble

Who wants trouble to plague his/her life? I can't think of one person that I have ever met who fits this description. Of course, there are people who seem to have trouble no matter where they go or what they do. I heard a woman say that trouble follows her son around. This was because no matter what he was doing wrong, a police officer seemed to always show up. If he was driving without a proper license, a police officer would stop him.

Most of us don't experience trouble to that extent; however, we have had our share of troubles in our lives. The important thing about trouble is how we handle it. It is very important who you look to during the time of trouble.

Friends and family are appropriate examples of who you can look to when trouble shows up in your life. Many times, you can draw trouble to yourself by being disobedient and careless. Nevertheless, the appropriate response to trouble is very important. The appropriate response is to ask the Lord to show you what the lesson is in the situation, and how you can be a better person.

What The Bible Says About Trouble

(Just a few scriptures)

John 16:33 (ESV)
I have said these things to you, that in me you may have peace. In the world you will have tribulation. But take heart; I have overcome the world.

2 Timothy 3:1-5 (ESV)
But understand this, that in the last days there will come times of difficulty.
For people will be lovers of self, lovers of money, proud, arrogant, abusive, disobedient to their parents, ungrateful, unholy, heartless, unappeasable, slanderous, without self-control, brutal, not loving good, treacherous, reckless, swollen with conceit, lovers of pleasure rather than lovers of God, having the appearance of godliness, but denying its power. Avoid such people....

Matthew 6:24-26 (ESV)
No one can serve two masters, for either he will hate the one and love the other, or he will be devoted to the one and despise the other. You cannot serve God and money.
Therefore I tell you, do not be anxious about your life, what you will eat or what you will drink, nor about your body, what you will put on. Is not life more than food, and the body more than clothing?
Look at the birds of the air: they neither sow nor reap nor gather into barns, and yet your heavenly Father feeds them. Are you not of more value than they?

Jesus, understood that we would have trouble. He himself experienced trouble while completing His assignment here on earth. He was acquainted with everything that we experience today. He was lied on, beaten, spat on and accused of many other unimaginable things.

Who are we that we should not face trouble? The good news, as I have mentioned above, is that trouble does not last always. You can make it. You can take it. You can overcome any obstacle in your life.

7

God Is Faithful

In mid-March I returned to the cancer center to continue my chemo sessions. This was going to be the 2nd five-day session. My mind was heavily focused on whether this session would end up with me in the hospital for another five weeks, which happened with the first session. I was praying that this would not be the case. I was concerned but my faith was keeping me strong, and I was believing God would see me through.

I continuously played my praise CDs all through the day and night, which allowed me to be filled with peace. I also continuously read healing scriptures out loud to myself, which kept my faith at a high level.

The book of healing scriptures was still one of my constant companions. When you are going through the storm, and when you are seeking healing in any way, you must praise God like never. I always tell people that you cannot wait until you are in the fire or the storm to begin to praise God or have faith — you must practice this in your daily life. I had been saved at that time for thirty-one years and it helped to prepare me for this fiery furnace. I had no idea though that the furnace was about to get even hotter, and that my faith would continue to be tested in a big way.

The first four days of chemo were difficult. I still slept a lot, and did not have an appetite. I was in severe pain when not heavily medicated.

Since I am asthmatic, the medicines that were being administered to me caused my asthma to flare up. My roommate's family advised the nurses that I was severely wheezing and was having a difficult time.

Besides this, my vital signs had begun to go to a high level. By the fourth day of chemo my entire body was out of whack. I had no idea exactly what was happening to me at that time. The chemo side effects caused me to need blood and platelet transfusions. I was in and out of tests, scans, x-rays, MRI's and the works.

My family and nurses noticed that I was not talking sensibly. Somehow, I knew that I was not alright. Several times a day nurses and doctors asked me questions to determine my state of mind. They posed questions such as, "What day and year is it?" "Who is the president of the United States?" "What is your first and last name?" I found myself trying to think of the answers, but they would not come to my mind. My sister said I gave the medical staff her name instead of mine. I could not give my address or much less any other personal information.

It was determined that I was suffering from delirium (An acutely disturbed state of mind that occurs in fever, intoxication, and other disorders and is characterized by restlessness, illusions, and incoherence of thought and speech). The doctors explained that this condition happens to one out of every three patients who are given the same chemo treatment for sarcoma tumors.

My family and nurses stated that I was extremely comical. Even though this medical condition was a serious matter, my family and medical staff laughed at many things that I said and did. I heard one nurse say, "This is the funniest patient we have ever had." I come from a family of very comical people, but I have never considered myself to be such. I guess that side of me showed up.

I remember most of the things I did during that awful period. After it was over my twin nieces, Kami and Kayli, reminded me of all of it. I remember when my nephew, Orondi and his wife Angelique, came to visit me from Atlanta. They had attended a special event and was dressed nicely. I sat up and called Angelique, *Oprah Winfrey.* They laughed and laughed about this. In my mind I knew she was not Oprah. Her hair was fixed very nicely, and she did remind me of Oprah. Therefore, it was a joke to me to refer to her as Oprah. They assumed I said it due to my delirium.

Divine Favor

Throughout all of this, I know that the Lord was on my side. While I was in this state of delirium, the medical staff had to place my bed on lock down with an alarm. God showed me favor in so many ways. I was placed in a private room with a twenty-four-hour nurse by my side. My bed continued to be locked for fear that I could harm myself in the state I was in. I understood what was going on but not with a clear mind.

The private room I was placed in was totally ordained by God because it was actually a unit that looked like a nice hotel. It was for patients who were receiving bone marrow transplants and was available at that time. Medically speaking, I needed this special attention. I am not sure how I would have recovered without this careful treatment.

Also, I remember when I was in the special unit, my pastor and some church members came to visit me. I was somewhat coming out of the delirium. I started telling them of a song I had been listening to on a CD. I was especially giving instructions to Randall, one of my church members who is a musician. I was trying to tell him how to play the song, but was very overboard in my instructions. That's one of the things we laughed about later.

I never discussed other details of what I was experiencing even to this day. During my time of confinement, I remember having illusions. At one point, I thought that a piece of my thigh had fallen off, and that no one was telling me about it. Since the cancerous tumor was in the hamstring area, I could not see what was going on.

I faintly recall asking the nurses, "Why are you laughing at me?" as I was going in and out of sleep" I was so bad off at one point that I could hear the nurses saying that they needed to keep me awake, so they kept shaking me as I would try to fall asleep. No one will ever know exactly what a horrific experience this was unless they have been through something similar.

My vital signs continued to escalate and to put it frankly, I was at death's door. But God! My appetite was getting worse by the day. My sister and my nieces were worried that I would remain in the delirious state of mind after everything was over. The doctors assured them that my mind would return to normal after about three days, and it did. I was then placed back into a regular room.

I wondered if it could get any worse than this. I thought about those words from Rev. Dr. McKinnon, *"It will seem like death, but it is only a shadow."* I also thought back on a conversation that Reverend Vickers and I had before I started the cancer treatments. He had come to my residence one day and ministered to me. He said that I was going to go through something extremely hard during my treatments. He said I needed to just keep the faith through it all. I remember thinking to myself that I already knew this would be hard. However, I later realized that what he ministered to me about was everything I went through regarding the delirium and near-death experience.

The doctors explained to me that because my body reacted badly to the ingredients in the chemo (which was specialized for sarcoma tumors) that they would not be able to continue my remaining three chemo sessions. They informed me that I would have to go through surgery as the next step in my journey. I was not sure if I was relieved. I just knew I was still praising God the best that I knew how.

Did You Come Forth As Pure Gold?

1 Peter 1:7
That the trial of your faith, being much more precious than of gold that perisheth, though it be tried with fire, might be found unto praise and honour and glory at the appearing of Jesus Christ.

The Apostle Paul was very aware of what the believers were going through. He understood that there are seasons in every Christian's life when they must have afflictions. A Christian must go through all types of trials, temptations, and situations. Paul also understood that a Christian must stand strong in the midst of trials and afflictions. He was no stranger to affliction himself as expressed in his writings.

2 Corinthians 11:23-27 (NLT)
Are they servants of Christ? I know I sound like a madman, but I have served him far more! I have worked harder, been put in prison more often, been whipped times without number, and faced death again and again.
Five different times the Jewish leaders gave me thirty-nine lashes. Three times I was beaten with rods. Once I was stoned. Three times I was shipwrecked. Once I spent a whole night and a day adrift at sea. I have traveled on many long journeys. I have faced danger from rivers and from robbers. I have faced danger from my own people, the Jews, as well as from the Gentiles. I have faced danger in the cities, in the deserts, and on the seas. And I have faced danger from men who claim to be believers but are not.
I have worked hard and long, enduring many sleepless nights. I have been hungry and thirsty and have often gone without food.

I have shivered in the cold, without enough clothing to keep me warm.

Paul had surely been in and through the fire. There is one account in Acts 28th chapter where he was bitten by a venomous snake and survived. Paul was on his way to Rome to stand trial before Caesar. In the previous chapter 27, he and those traveling with him were caught in a very bad storm. Everyone, except Paul, believed that they were not going to survive. The Lord sent an angel to comfort Paul and to tell him that the ship would be lost, but that all the lives of those on the ship would be spared.

They really went through a lot and their ship was lost in the storm. Paul continued to believe that the Lord would bring them through and they all made it safely to the shore. Paul and his shipmates became marooned on an island named Melita. When they landed, they were met by some very friendly natives who offered them assistance.

As Paul was helping gather wood for the fire, he laid a bundle of sticks in the flames. At that time, a viper came out of the wood and bit him. Paul cast the snake into the fire. The natives were all waiting for something dreadful to happen to Paul, but Paul survived. God took care of Paul as He had done many times before.

You may wonder why God would allow Paul to go through something like this snake bite. Many times, your fire experience comes after you have done good for others. Even though you have served God faithfully, as Paul had, you will still have to go through a fire experience.

Refine Me Lord

God wants to refine us, which can mean to reduce to a pure state. Besides, it can mean to be free from moral imperfection, or it can mean to improve by pruning or polishing. In our walk with the Lord, we too must be refined. The only way our character can be refined is by walking through certain situations. God tries our faith, our trust and our belief in Him as the true and living God. It is in situations such as the one that I was experiencing that God can get the glory out of our lives. Let's look at the refining process of gold, which is referenced in the Bible several times.

There are different methods of refining gold. Gold can be refined either by using a flame in high temperatures or by using chemicals. The Word of God references the refining process with the flame of fire. In ancient times, this refining process involved a craftsman who would sit next to a fire, and the process used would remove impurities. Gold will not get to its desirable state without the processes mentioned above.

If we never have troubles or problems, how will we know whether God can solve them? If we never have sickness, or what Paul may have referred to as a thorn in the flesh, how will we ever know that God can heal? By no means am I suggesting that God gives us sickness, as Jesus bore it all for our sicknesses as well as our Salvation. I also realize that some Christians are afraid to claim a sickness because there are those who will say they have no faith. There are some who scold others about claiming a sickness.

In 1980-1981 I was a part of the Florida Mass Choir. We recorded a song entitled *"Have You Been Tried in the Fire?"* This is a valid question. The song then asks a secondary question, *"Did you come forth as pure gold?"* This song is a great reminder that it is not enough to be tried in the fire, but you must pass the test and come through as pure gold.

In my situation, I knew my illness was real. The excruciating pain was a constant reminder. It was real! I had a real tumor that I had not been able to pray away. I had prayed and prayed prior to starting treatments. I had faith that I could be healed without going through any procedures. I believed that I could lay hands on myself and the tumor would go away.

A friend of mine asked a certain prophet to call me, and I spoke with him with an expectation of what the Lord could do before I started the cancer process. He had told me of his experience praying for many people with tumors. He said that I would be healed.

I had no problem believing that at all, but now I found myself in the middle of chemo treatments that failed and facing a surgery to remedy the situation. We will never fully understand God's ways. His ways are past finding out. It behooves us to take Him at His word and believe that we are overcomers. We are victorious.

8

Waiting Is Not Easy

There are many accounts of miracles in the Bible. In the New Testament, Jesus went about doing good. His ministry on earth gave hope and peace to many lost and hurting people. He healed and did many miracles in His own way and time.

Many of us do not understand the timing of God. We live in a "microwave" society. We are used to popping a food item in the microwave oven for seconds or minutes. If we are super hungry, we do not have to cook a meal in the oven, or on top of the stove. Sometimes it is not even a matter of hunger; we may just be tired and weary from the day.

So many women now work outside of the home. Some husbands still expect women to come home from work, deal with the children if any, and prepare a full course meal. Then there are other men who use teamwork to make their household run smoothly.

Many people, even Christians, are used to having things their way. When you give your life to the Lord, your way should be yielded to what God wants to do in your life. When you are going through a trial of any kind, sometimes it may be difficult to rest in God and wait on Him.

During my battle with cancer, I was looking for my faith to fix my situation without having to go through much of anything. I prayed and prayed that the lump on my hamstring was nothing serious. After I was mistakenly told that the swelling was a hematoma, and the cancerous tumor was confirmed, then I asked God to allow someone to lay hands on me and make the tumor disappear. I wondered why it was a problem to expect this as I had read the Bible stories over and over in my years as a Born-Again Christian. I had seen the miracles— so why would God not do it for me, a faithful servant? I believe one answer is found in this scripture:

James 1:3-4
Knowing this, that the trying of your faith worketh patience. But let patience have her perfect work, that ye may be perfect and entire, wanting nothing.

A Counterfeit

We must have patience. During many situations in our lives God is testing our faith and our patience. He wants to know if we can stand in the time of our trial. I can relate to this in so many ways. As a single woman, I do not understand why I have never married. Marriage is something I desired at an early age.

The only prerequisite to me getting married was a high school and college education. I achieved the latter in 1979, by earning my B.A. Degree from the University of South Florida. So, what is the hold up? This is a question that many other Christian single women and men have asked.

When I received Christ in my life at the age of twenty-four, I made a vow to myself that I would not be in and out of relationships. I felt that if I was going to live that lifestyle then there was no need for me to get saved. I became involved in ministry shortly after I dedicated my life to the Lord. Although I was tested and feel that I failed on some accounts by getting involved in a few unequally yoked relationships, I have mainly been proud of my walk with Christ.

I have had a few marriage proposals that I knew was not of God. After I accepted Christ in 1981, a group of my co-workers and I began to have Bible study during our lunch hour. One of the leaders of our group was a preacher who worked as a maintenance man on my job. He was older than I and the others, but we highly respected him. One day he came to my office and told me he needed to talk. I welcomed him into my office, having no idea what it was all about.

He began to tell me that the Lord had told him I was his wife. Those words hit my ears like someone lighting a firecracker right in front of me. I was speechless. I had only known him for a short time and even though I was a new babe in Christ, I had great discernment. I searched my mind for what to say and nothing, absolutely nothing, came out of my mouth. He finally told me to think and pray about it then left my office.

God knows I wanted to be married. I had no real restrictions at that time. I had a full-time job and I was college educated. I also had no children. Nevertheless, something inside of me knew that this was just not right! I immediately began to ask God what I should do.

I did not want to go to anyone to talk about this situation just yet. The only thing I knew to do was avoid him at all costs. So, for the next couple of weeks I did just that. I ducked and dodged him to the best of my ability. I wondered why he had to ruin a perfectly good friendship. What was worse was that he was a man of the cloth, a preacher, a servant of God. I simply did not understand this situation at all.

I finally spoke to my ministries' Bible study teacher about it. I was given wisdom on the situation. I was still not about to seek this man out to tell him of my decision, but at the same time I decided that I would not run from him any longer. I felt that he had to know this was just not of God.

After about two weeks of avoiding him, he appeared in my office. I had rehearsed what I would tell him. There was a moment of silence between us. Then he began to speak. "I came to apologize to you. God did not tell me that you are my wife. I was in my flesh, and I am the one who wanted it to happen," he said.

It was like time stood still. I looked at him, studying him closer than I had ever done before. His age showed more than ever even though he was a good-looking man. He was not well-spoken and seemed to have very little education. I don't think I had really paid much attention to any of that before since I was not the type of person to shun people. However; by now, it was clear to me that we were a total mismatch. I was so relieved. I smiled and told him it was alright and that I wanted to remain friends. Even though I said that to him, things were simply awkward between us after that!

When the Devil knows that you are waiting for something he sometimes put a counterfeit in the way. Sometimes if we are tired of waiting we can accept something that is far from what God has for us. For example, regarding a terminal illness, we can accept death instead of life.

I also remember that before I gave my life to the Lord, I was dating a very nice man. He was intelligent and educated, quite different from the preacher who had asked me to marry him. This man already owned a home and maintained a good job. Unfortunately for this person, he met me at a time when I was very conflicted. I had been having dreams about the Rapture as well as other dreams from a young age. I knew the Lord's hand was on my life. At the time I met this man, my life was being shaken. I was running from the Lord. I wanted very much to be saved, but I allowed the cares of life to trip me up as many young women do. We became involved in a relationship after a short time knowing each other.

I felt that he cared deeply for me. During that time, I spoke often of my plans to give my life to the Lord. I really had been telling my friends this for a long time. I was experiencing some things that I knew was a result of my running from the Lord's will. One day my boyfriend told me he needed to leave for several weeks for his duties in the Army National Guard. I knew within myself that things might be different when he returned.

While he was gone I became so fed up with myself that I went into my office at work, closed my door and prayed the prayer of Salvation from a little book that was given to me by an elderly woman on my job, who also had given me a Bible. I knew she was being led by God, but at the time she had given me these things I felt that she had plenty of nerves to do so. I felt that she did not know me well enough. On that day in June of 1981, I felt so good with my new life. When I walked outside, everything looked different. I felt different. God had done something in my heart, and I knew it.

One day not long after I received Christ as my Savior, I was returning to my apartment in Ft. Lauderdale, Florida from my sister's home in Pompano Beach. I was waiting for the traffic light to turn green, so I could make a left onto Interstate 95 going south. Suddenly, I heard an audible voice in my car. At first it was soft and undemanding. The voice said, "Janice you need to go break up with (boyfriend's name) now." I did not know what was going on. I had never heard a voice like this before. I was still sitting at the traffic light when the voice spoke again.

This time it was louder and more demanding. The voice repeated the same thing again, but this time with more force. Before I could think much about what was going on my car began to move on its own. There was a median strip to the left of me. My car slowly began turning on its own, turning into the other lane -– going back toward the way I was traveling from.

The amazing thing is my boyfriend's home was in that direction even though I was not coming from his home at that time. It was as if my car was being pushed by men (as it happens when a car runs out of gas), out of the road. I looked in my rear-view mirror and saw a woman behind me who was looking like she was amazed at what was happening. I have no idea if she was seeing an angel pushing my car or just what was going on. My car eventually stopped.

Since I was new in the Lord, I did not understand what was going on. I assumed that this was the Devil. As soon as I could take control of my car

I turned it around and continued to my apartment. I kept this incident to myself. I knew most people would not believe this happened to me. I also did not immediately share it with my boyfriend.

At that time, I was very involved in a ministry that required a group of friends and myself to travel from Ft. Lauderdale to Miami each week. My boyfriend, who was usually an understanding person, began to get annoyed with me more and more. He simply did not understand why I felt the need to drive or ride so far just for church. He had begun to badger me about it. I often thought of the audible voice and the experience I had in the car that day, and wondered if I should share it with him.

By now, I knew that the Lord was telling me to end my relationship with this man. I was reluctant because I really did not want to hurt his feelings. At this point, I had pulled away from the close relationship that we had previously.

Then one weekend night my roommate decided to give a party for her sister at our apartment. She asked me if I would pick up her sister and bring her to the party. My boyfriend became unusually annoyed and began to complain about it. I had had enough! I told him it was time to break up. I then shared the story of what happened to me in the car that day. I told him that I believed the Lord had spoken to me in an audible voice, etc.

I also told him I should have followed God's command to me weeks before that, but that I was ready to do so. That was the end of the relationship. I knew even though waiting was difficult, I had to learn to wait on the Lord in every aspect of my life. Now, waiting on a healing was a new phase of my life. I had no choice but to wait for God to move.

Preparing For A Miracle

Yes, I had my experiences with waiting, but now this was the longest wait of all. I was at my sister's home most of the time during this cancer journey, but sometimes would return to my place of residence in Miami to give her a break. She did not ask me to do this, but I felt it was necessary. Dr. Temple, my Orthopedic Surgeon at UMHC informed me that he would proceed with surgery to remove the tumor from my hamstring. It was indeed a long wait, and now the time had come for me to report to the hospital for the surgery.

It was April 4, 2012. Some of my siblings and a nephew had come to Miami to support me. I knew this was very hard for them after the death of my mother and sister. I knew they were very concerned with what the outcome would be.

My sister Peggy and I, reported to the hospital early on the morning of the surgery. I had prayed and prayed for God to take me through this. Doctors had explained that since the type of tumor I had required two types of radiation, the doctor would be present during the surgery to place radioactive implants in my leg.

This action was for a future radiation treatment called Brachytherapy, which is the treatment of cancer done by inserting radioactive implants directly into the tissue. It was explained to me that after all the sessions of this procedure was completed, I would then go through External Beam Radiation.

I had no idea how I would make it through all of this, but I was still standing strong in my faith. I knew that if God had brought me to that place, He could and would take me all the way. In my spirit, I could hear the famous gospel singer, Reverend James Cleveland, singing the song "I Don't Feel No Ways Tired."

I mainly focused on the refrain of this song, *"I don't believe He brought me this far to leave me."* I could not honestly say that I did not feel tired. I was very tired. I was tired of feeling sick. I was tired of being in pain. I was tired of no appetite, or all food tasting like poison. I was tired of being pricked with needles. I was tired of the PICC lines being infected and having to be changed frequently. Yes, I was tired!

Even though I was tired, I was so very grateful for what the Lord had done for me. I knew I could have been dead. I knew the tumor could have been found in the last stage instead of when it appeared on my leg. I knew I could have been in a place that did not have the excellent medical care that I was receiving. Yes, I was tired, but I had come too far from where I started from! I was believing God for a miracle.

I had read many accounts in the Bible where ordinary people received unexpected miracles. There were many who came to Jesus with great expectation such as the woman with the issue of blood, or the centurion soldier, etc. There was the first miracle when Jesus turned the water into wine at the wedding.

The mother of Jesus knew that her son was special and that He had a purpose. She knew He could do something to help this wedding be successful for the bride and groom. This is the reason she called on Jesus at the time of need.

Mary had experienced a miracle of her own, which was the birth of Jesus. She had not seen Jesus himself perform a miracle before this wedding, but it was time for God's will to be manifested through Him. She knew that He indeed had a destiny to fulfill, and a purpose.

John 2:1-11

And the third day there was a marriage in Cana of Galilee; and the mother of Jesus was there:

And both Jesus was called, and his disciples, to the marriage.

And when they wanted wine, the mother of Jesus saith unto him, They have no wine.

Jesus saith unto her, Woman, what have I to do with thee? mine hour is not yet come.

His mother saith unto the servants, Whatsoever he saith unto you, do it. And there were set there six waterpots of stone, after the manner of the purifying of the Jews, containing two or three firkins apiece.

Jesus saith unto them, Fill the waterpots with water. And they filled them up to the brim.

And he saith unto them, Draw out now, and bear unto the governor of the feast. And they bare it.

When the ruler of the feast had tasted the water that was made wine, and knew not whence it was: (but the servants which drew the water knew;) the governor of the feast called the bridegroom,

And saith unto him, Every man at the beginning doth set forth good wine; and when men have well drunk, then that which is worse: but thou hast kept the good wine until now.

This beginning of miracles did Jesus in Cana of Galilee, and manifested forth his glory; and his disciples believed on him.

In my case, I had seen miracles in my own life as well as others. I was expecting God to come through for me in surgery, but I had no idea what I was about to encounter. I had no idea of just how much I was going to need a miracle, but I would soon find out!

Let This Cup Pass From Me

I had prayed for months and weeks for God to let this cup pass from me. Jesus prayed this prayer in Matthew 26:38-39.

Then saith he unto them, My soul is exceeding sorrowful, even unto death: tarry ye here, and watch with me.

And he went a little farther, and fell on his face, and prayed, saying, O my Father, if it be possible, let this cup pass from me: nevertheless not as I will, but as thou wilt.

Yes, I wanted this problem to go away. I had already been through a lot. I knew God had been with me all the way through, but now I wanted Him to just touch me and make it all disappear. I knew I could not compare myself to Jesus, but I found myself trying to imagine what it must have been like to know that you were about to sacrifice your life for others.

In my case, I knew that cancer was a life-threatening disease. I knew that many people did not survive. I had also learned that years ago, there was no real way to treat sarcoma tumors and many had to have their limbs amputated or did not survive.

Even though I was aware of all of this, and surely did not want to experience any further suffering, I felt the peace of God. I had braced myself for whatever it was that I must go through if the Lord allowed me to go through.

The Vision

Somewhere in the process of my journey, I remembered a vision that the Lord gave me in 1983 when I moved to Miami. At that time, I was rooming with two friends in my ministry, Robin and Vera. Robin was now, in 2012, the First Lady of my church. Shortly after I moved in with them in 1983, I was lying in the bed one night but had not yet fallen asleep. Suddenly, as I lay awake, I saw a scene appear above my head.

This scene was a group of medical doctors standing over me in a hospital bed. They appeared to be operating on me, but I could not determine what they were doing exactly, or what part of my body was affected. At that time, I heard an audible voice speak loudly to me. "This is not a sickness until death, but it is all for my GLORY." Other than the story that I shared earlier about the audible voice that told me to break up with my boyfriend, I had not heard a voice like this.

I had certainly never had an open vision. I was shaken by this occurrence. Somehow though I did not feel afraid. I surmised that God was indeed speaking to me about something that was going to happen to me in the future. I shared this event with absolutely no one at that time. I kept this in my spirit, and any time I was ill in any way I silently wondered was it going to be the time that the vision had forewarned me of.

Prayer Makes A Difference

As I lay awake in the hospital pre-operation room on April 4th I wondered was this the entire experience that the Lord had spoken to me about? I was surrounded by nurses preparing me for my surgery. I felt a peace, God's peace, but how was I to know what was about to come? I was very glad my family was there. We are a close and praying family. I expected nothing less than for my siblings and nephew to offer up a prayer to the Lord on my behalf.

Praying has a calming effect. I was so pleased that I had every one of them standing over my bed. That is what family is for, to be there in the time of each other's need. This is what my family was used to. Our mom always preached to us to be there for each other. When a family member is in the hospital, especially in an emergency, we usually crowd the hospital waiting room, etc.

Prayer is an essential part of a Christian's walk with God. Prayer has many benefits. The Bible tells us to pray without ceasing. Philippians 4:6 says: Be careful for nothing; but in every thing by prayer and supplication with thanksgiving let your requests be made known unto God.

I had surely let my requests be known to God from the first day that I was diagnosed with cancer. It was no different on this day. I had awakened very early and prayed to my Lord and Savior Jesus Christ, to protect me and bring me through this crucial surgery.

By the time my family finished praying with me, Dr. Temple came in. I noticed a different look on his face. From the time that I had met him, he was always pleasant and kind. He was always able to ensure me that I was in good hands.

On that morning, he looked very concerned and I finally asked him if everything was okay. He explained that from all the images taken it was obvious that the nerves were wrapped around the tumor. He said it was going to be a complicated surgery. He then mentioned that there would be quite a few doctors in the OR with him and that he did not know exactly what could be done.

Before I could react at all, my sister Geraldine, who is also a minister and a powerful woman of God, spoke out on my behalf. She said, "Why don't you just take Jesus in the room with you." I remember clearly that Dr. Temple's face lit up. He responded, "That's a very good person to take in there." This is all I remember because the anesthesia soon kicked in.

Hours later, I woke up from surgery not knowing what the outcome was. All I knew was that I was alive. Yes, alive! All I knew was that my God had not failed to take me through the surgery. He had not failed to wake me up. He had not failed to give me another chance at life. That is all I knew, but there was so much more.

After recovery, I was admitted to the UMHC Hospital for recuperation. I felt so strange when I looked down at my thigh and saw needles for the Brachytherapy (internal radiation) that I described earlier. This is what the radiation oncologist had explained to me before my surgery. He had advised that immediately after I was discharged from the hospital, I would be reporting to him to begin this procedure.

I absolutely could not move my right leg. I was in severe pain and had to be heavily medicated. For the first few days I could not get out of the bed on my own for the restroom or anything. I had a large boot on my leg and foot. I remember feeling somewhat fearful about the inability to move my leg.

I had thought to myself "What if something happens in the hospital such as a fire or other emergency?" My mind was working overtime thinking that I would be at the mercy of someone else to move me or take me out of harm's way. It was a feeling that I never had before.

I was used to my independence, but now I had no choice but to lie there. This was my state for a short time until the therapist began to come and walk me to the restroom. Then the therapist started walking me down the hallway. It was a task that seemed impossible, but slowly I could make steps with the help of medical staff. I had to keep telling myself that I could do all things through Christ that strengthens me, per the Word of God.

My pastor, Reverend Vickers, came to visit me one evening while I was in the hospital. This was just a few days after the surgery. He told me that my testimony was shared with our congregation at church on that past Sunday. He said everyone praised God for the miracle that I had received.

I had a strange look on my face and he asked me what was wrong. I said to him "Reverend Vickers I don't even know what happened." I told him that every time someone had started to tell me about the surgery, I changed the subject. I guess I had not been ready to hear it at all. All I knew was that the resident doctors were coming every day to change my bandages, etc.

The doctors had not yet given me a medical explanation of what happened in that OR. Reverend Vickers looked at me in amazement. "You really don't know?" He asked. I told him that I really didn't know. He began to explain to me what happened, and the miracle I received in surgery to remove the cancerous tumor from my right hamstring. He said your family told me all about it and I shared it with everyone.

I felt tears welling up in my eyes. I knew it was a serious matter, and that my life was at stake, but I had not thought of what could have possibly gone on in that room. I did know that I had prayed for God to release his angels in that room, and for the healing hands of Jesus to touch me in a mighty way. God answers prayers.

9

Discouragement

I mentioned previously that there was only one time that I remember feeling completely discouraged throughout my cancer journey. At that time, I called my pastor and told him I was not going to do treatments of any kind. He counseled me through my discouragement, and I was ready to fight the battle again.

Many times, we get discouraged while going through life's battles. We are human, and in those situations, we can find an excuse for why we feel the way we do. However, discouragement is not God's plan for our lives. There are times when we bring situations on ourselves. We step outside of God's will for us, which often results in us being discouraged.

The definition of discouragement in the dictionary is "A loss of confidence or enthusiasm." Yes, we tend to let our situations cause us to lose confidence in something that we once believed in. The Devil uses discouragement to get us off track. During those times, we must be wise enough to discern the trick of the enemy.

You can let discouragement set in when you are going through a job loss, a divorce, singlehood, inability to bear a child and many other circumstances. You begin to say to yourself, "This situation is never going to get better." You ask yourself "Why should I keep trying or believing?" During these times, you must grab hold to faith and believe like never before.

The way you handle discouragement can be the difference between life and death. You can allow situations to make you compromise the Word of God, and obey the Devil instead of your Almighty God. When we compromise, we can make the wrong decisions. Therefore, we must fight discouragement with all our might. This takes the help of God as we cannot fight the battles of life on our own.

If you think hard enough, even in your Christian journey, you can remember a time of discouragement in your life. Ask yourself, what lead to this feeling of hopelessness or doubt? Go back down memory lane and you will likely find that there were times when you did not follow God's instructions. You veered to the left when He said go right, or vice versa.

In a case of illness, such as I was experiencing, the doctors told me that there is no evidence for the cause of sarcoma cancer. Therefore, at the point of my diagnosis and treatments I could not keep beating myself up about how this happened to me. Sure, I could have eaten better, exercised more, taken better care of myself, etc. When all those things are done perfectly—some diseases are still not prevented.

The test for me was to believe God, trust Him, and follow every step that doctors were now giving me to get to the desired end, which was to survive cancer. Discouragement had no place in my life at that time nor the present.

Intense Prayer

I have already spoken on prayer. If you don't know anything else to do, you can always lean on prayer. Many times, we feel that God already knows how we feel so why should we bother to talk to Him. Remember that prayer is just talking to God. You can talk to Him like you talk to your best friend, but of course God knows everything about you—*even the secrets that you have not shared with anyone else. Prayer changes things!*

During my illness, I prayed a lot. Of course, I was glad that others were praying for me, but I knew I had to talk to God for myself. Even when I may not have thought I was discouraged, God knew exactly how I was feeling. He knows all about us.

I am so glad that we have a wonderful God, and there is no other God like Him. As a matter of fact, you must believe that He is the only true and living God. God rewards those who seek Him with their whole heart. In times of trouble, seeking Him is not an option, but *necessary.*

King David And Ziklag

What I love about the Bible, the infallible Word of God, is that there are accounts of many who went through situations like ours. One of the greatest examples of discouragement is found in 1 Samuel 27-30. In this story, King David faced great discouragement.

In prior scriptures, David had spent much of his time running from King Saul. Saul was determined to kill David, as he felt David was a threat to his throne. God had chosen David to be the king of Israel. After about ten years of escaping Saul, David finally decided to go to the land of the Philistines to get away in peace.

In other words, David became hopeless. He moved outside of the will of God. God had promised him that he would be the king of Israel. When God makes a promise, the promise is sure. This is what happens when we take matters into our own hand and try to fix things ourselves. Out of all the victories that God had given David, one after another, it seems he forgot that he was victorious.

We have seen God come through for us time and time again. We have gotten the victory in many situations in our lives, yet we decide that we cannot run on any longer. David made this decision out of frustration and weariness. This is when the enemy can really trap us, during a time when we become weary and worn.

Remember in his young life, David had previously gotten the victory over the giant Goliath, who was a Philistine. God had allowed David and his army to conquer many lands. So now, David surmised that he could go to the land of the Philistines, and Saul would not come after him anymore.

It is understandable how David may have felt. There are times in our lives when we have been fighting a battle for a very long time. Our only solution, according to us, is to just end the situation by going to a different place or a making a different choice.

In 1 Samuel 27:1-7 (NLT) it is explained what happened when David relocated:

So David took his 600 men and went over and joined Achish son of Maoch, the king of Gath.
David and his men and their families settled there with Achish at Gath. David brought his two wives along with him—Ahinoam from Jezreel and Abigail, Nabal's widow from Carmel.
Word soon reached Saul that David had fled to Gath, so he stopped hunting for him.
One day David said to Achish, "If it is all right with you, we would rather live in one of the country towns instead of here in the royal city."
So Achish gave him the town of Ziklag (which still belongs to the kings of Judah to this day), and they lived there among the philistines for a year and four months.

The problem occurred when Achish ordered David and his men to fight with them against Israel. Now with all Achish had done for him, David felt he had to compromise and join him in the battle. In 1 Samuel 29:1-11

(NLT), it explains what happened after David agreed to go to battle against the Israelites, where Saul was the King.

The entire Philistine army now mobilized at Aphek, and the Israelites camped at the spring in Jezreel.

As the Philistine rulers were leading out their troops in groups of hundreds and thousands, David and his men marched at the rear with King Achish.

But the Philistine commanders demanded, "What are these Hebrews doing here?" And Achish told them, "This is David, the servant of King Saul of Israel. He's been with me for years, and I've never found a single fault in him from the day he arrived until today."

But the Philistine commanders were angry. "Send him back to the town you've given him!" they demanded. "He can't go into the battle with us.

What if he turns against us in battle and becomes our adversary? Is there any better way for him to reconcile himself with his master than by handing our heads over to him?

Isn't this the same David about whom the women of Israel sing in their dances, 'Saul has killed his thousands, and David his ten thousands'?"

So Achish finally summoned David and said to him, "I swear by the LORD that you have been a trustworthy ally. I think you should go with me into battle, for I've never found a single flaw in you from the day you arrived until today. But the other Philistine rulers won't hear of it.

Please don't upset them, but go back quietly."

"What have I done to deserve this treatment?" David demanded. "What have you ever found in your servant, that I can't go and fight the enemies of my lord the king?"

But Achish insisted, "As far as I'm concerned, you're as perfect as an angel of God. But the Philistine commanders are afraid to have you with them in the battle.
Now get up early in the morning, and leave with your men as soon as it gets light."
So David and his men headed back into the land of the Philistines, while the Philistine army went on to Jezreel.

This is when trouble really started for David. 1 Samuel 30th chapter, tells the story of what happened when David and his men returned to Ziklag, three days later. They found that the Amalekites had made a raid into the Negev and Ziklag; and they had crushed Ziklag and burned it to the ground. They had also carried off the women and children, and everyone else, but had not killed any of David's people.

When David and his men saw what had happened to their families, they wept a lot. David's two wives, Ahinoam and Abigail, were in the group of people that were captured. The men were very upset about the loss of their families, and began to talk about stoning David. David had to strengthen himself in the Lord.

David asked the Lord if he should chase after the raiders and the Lord told him, "Yes." David took men along with him. They ended up finding an Egyptian in the field, who was a slave of an Amalekite— the people who had raided David's territory. The man led them to where the Amalekites were eating, drinking and dancing in celebration of all the plunder they had gotten from the raid.

David and his men rushed in among them and slaughtered them throughout that night and the entire next day until evening. None of the Amalekites were able to escape, except 400 young men who fled on camels. The conclusion was that David got back everything the Amalekites had taken from them, including his two wives.

A Great Lesson

There is a great lesson in this story for all of us. The key is that after all of this happened, David found strength in His God. This is the same God that he had written many psalms about. This is the God that forgave him when he committed adultery with Bathsheba. Sometimes we forget what the Lord has done in our lives, and how He brought us through many trials and tribulations in times past.

We must learn that we cannot depend on our own strength. Trials come to make us strong. In my cancer journey, I did not want to give in to discouragement. This is the reason I continued to read my healing scriptures, and listen to my praise music. I knew too well that the enemy of my soul wanted to catch me off guard. He knew it was a devastating time in my life. He wanted me to curse God, as he tried to get Job to do.

I will never accept when people tell me that I was so strong, or that I am so strong. I know that my strength comes from the Lord. I knew then that I still had a long way to go, and I needed the Lord to take me all the way through. Only God could do this, and I was leaning and depending on Him.

10

Miracle In The Operating Room

I have seen and experienced miracles in my life as well as others. Some miracles in the Bible are more memorable than others. All of them are written to build our faith, and to let us know what our great God can do. This is one miracle in the Bible that quickly comes to my mind:

John 5:5-9
After this there was a feast of the Jews; and Jesus went up to Jerusalem.

Now there is at Jerusalem by the sheep market a pool, which is called in the Hebrew tongue Bethesda, having five porches.

In these lay a great multitude of impotent folk, of blind, halt, withered, waiting for the moving of the water.

For an angel went down at a certain season into the pool, and troubled the water: whosoever then first after the troubling of the water stepped in was made whole of whatsoever disease he had.

And a certain man was there, which had an infirmity thirty and eight years.

When Jesus saw him lie, and knew that he had been now a long time in that case, he saith unto him, Wilt thou be made whole?

The impotent man answered him, Sir, I have no man, when the water is troubled, to put me into the pool: but while I am coming, another steppeth down before me.

Jesus saith unto him, Rise, take up thy bed, and walk And immediately the man was made whole, and took up his bed, and walked: and on the same day was the sabbath.

I knew just as Jesus healed this lame man, He could heal me. However, I didn't know how or when He would do it. I had already gone through chemo, which was aborted due to severe side effects. All I knew was that I needed God to heal me through surgery.

The account of what happened in the OR during my surgery, was more than I could have imagined. It was explained to me that about two hours into the surgery, a doctor came out to the waiting room to talk to my family.

That doctor explained to my family that they were not able to talk with me about a decision that was needed during the surgery. He further explained that doctors had three options for the family to discuss on my behalf. The decision was whether to do one of the following options:

- Amputate my leg from my hip on down.
- Remove the sciatic nerve, which would result in me being confined to a wheel chair the rest of my life.
- Try to remove the tumor, but the cancer would most likely spread throughout my body.

My family was devastated with these options. (Remember that we lost my mother and sister months before this day.) I was told by my siblings that when they got the news from the doctor, they all began to pray and call other people to intercede on my behalf. They then expressed to the doctor their wish for them to do whatever option would save my life. The doctor went back to the OR.

After the long surgery was over, Dr. Temple came out to talk with my family. He reported, in his words, "We believe we saw a miracle in there today."

The account that my family relayed to me is as follows: After doctors had spoken to my family and went back into surgery, the nerves wrapped around the tumor seemed to move out of the way. There was also a clear line of demarcation which had allowed the tumor to stay in the right place, preventing cancer from spreading. Not only that, but the one and a half sessions of chemo that I had done prior to surgery had shrunk the tumor about 70 %.

Dr. Temple explained that doctors did not have to take any of the three options that were presented to my family, and they were able to remove the tumor. It was a detailed surgery. Doctors had to remove muscles, etc. He said the wound would take a long time to heal, and he was unable to predict the exact outcome regarding the full use of my leg. My family knew that God had come through for me in a miraculous way!

Who wouldn't serve a God like this? He is the Lord God of Abraham, Isaac and Jacob. I seemed so undeserving of a miracle such as this! Yes, I had faith that God would intervene, but I could never have written a story with an ending like this. I had praised God through this journey, but I was about to praise God like never.

The Devil had a plan for my death, but *God had a bigger plan for my life*. One of the scriptures I had repeated over and over throughout this whole journey was:

Psalm 118:17
I shall not die, but live, and declare the works of the Lord.

Thanks to the almighty God, I lived!

Prayer of Thanksgiving

Lord I am your child, and you promised to be with me always.
Thank you for all that you have done for me.
Thank you for not allowing the enemy to snatch
my life from me. I am eternally grateful

Prayer of Faithfulness

In my darkest struggle or most joyous times
dear Lord, help me
to be found faithful to you and to your will
In Jesus name, I pray.
Amen
Arthur Unknown

The Journey Continues

A little over a week after the surgery, the doctor told me that I needed to be discharged from UMHC hospital because I had to begin my Brachytherapy radiation treatments as soon as possible. I would only be able to go home for a day or two and then return to the UMHC Radiation Oncology department.

It was a struggle getting in and out of any vehicle. I still had the orthopedic boot on and could not even bend my leg. The surgery wound was from my hip down to below my knee (on the back of my thigh). Getting in and out of the bed was a feat. It was extremely difficult, but through the help of the Lord and my family, I knew I could make it.

I had made it from the beginning of my illness where I could not lie down on my right side at all. I could hardly sleep. I was miserable for a long time. It was the most excruciating pain I had ever experienced. I had made it to this point of my journey and I could not even think of not making it to the end.

The day I reported for the Brachytherapy radiation, my sister Peggy, had to push me in a wheelchair through the hospital. It was a long walk to the radiation oncology department. We finally made it there for my first appointment. The doctor and his staff explained the procedures they would be doing. I learned that I had to go into a small room alone. For some time, I had believed I was claustrophobic. This proved that I may have self-diagnosed myself correctly –- as I felt like I just could not do it.

For each session that lasted for a few weeks (not every day), the apparatus implanted in my thigh had to be connected to a machine. Each of the many needles protruding from my leg was placed one by one to the matching area on the radiation machine. This took time. After it was connected, I had to stay in a dimly lit room until the process was completed.

There were times when I wanted to scream out that it was enough. I was scolded a couple of times by the doctor who felt I was impatient and complaining. I felt I was doing very well based on the circumstances. I could not wait until this procedure was over and done with, and it soon was. One down and more to go! At least this part was finished, and I could brace myself for the next step.

I was allowed a break for a couple of weeks before the External Radiation started. Meanwhile, I was using a walker to get around. I was able to go on a few trips to the store with my sister. She and her husband continued to cook and do for me as needed. I was thankful that I could do some personal care for myself. A home health agency nurse came daily to assist me with certain shots and wound care. It was a trying time to say the least.

A couple of weeks later, it was time for me to return to the hospital for my next form of radiation. The Brachytherapy needles had been removed.

I reported to the first session at the UMHC radiation oncology office, and was relieved that it was being done in a much larger room. The machines looked humongous to me.

The same as the other radiation procedure, I had to lie flat on my stomach since the wound was on the back of my thigh. That had always been difficult for me. Staff had to make a mold the shape of my leg to do the treatments. My leg had to remain very still as the large machine passed around in the air sending radiation to the correct areas of my leg. Minutes seemed like an hour.

I reported certain days of the week for the radiation. The staff made it bearable as they were very friendly and caring. I was always glad when the machine would stop, and it was time for me to go. Weeks of radiation went by slowly, but I was finally given a certificate of completion. Staff wished me well, and told me they hoped I never had to return. I, too, hoped and prayed the same.

I had made it through chemo, two types of radiation, and surgery. I had been given several blood and platelet transfusions throughout the entire cancer process. Due to all the treatments, I still had issues with anemia. After one of the trips where I was brought back to my residence in Miami, I had no one to take me to the store near my home, so I drove myself there. I began to black out (faint) at the cash register, as I was very anemic.

Thank God that a quick thought came to my mind to take a puff of my asthma inhaler. Leaning over the checkout desk, I came back to myself and was able to get home. That incident landed me in the cancer center for a final platelet transfusion in July of 2012.

During this journey, I had gone from a wheelchair, to a walker, to crutches. The crutches had begun to affect my arms and my hands. I purchased the newer style millennial crutches which gave more relief for my arms. I continued to have issues of fluid retention in my leg and foot. It was necessary to always sit with my feet up during the day, and the purchase of a lift recliner chair was eventually a great decision.

Recuperation

During many follow-up visits with Dr. Temple, I found him to be such a kind and caring physician. My sister was always impressed with him. If I had to lie on the table and one of my shoes dropped on the floor, he would pick it up and put it on me. I remember one visit shortly after the surgery when he had to do an ultrasound. I had a small cyst that had appeared. I prayed and prayed that it was nothing to be concerned about. The ultrasound proved that it was nothing major.

He was always reassuring to me that I was fine. I appreciate having a physician who cares and treats patients with the utmost respect. Since the surgery, I had to do several sessions of physical therapy. None of the therapy worked well, because of the open wound I still had. Therapists were afraid to do much exercise with me for fear that the wound would open more. Also, I was still on crutches.

I was still suffering from pain and other effects of the surgery. Dr. Trent, Oncologist, explained that I needed to do some preventive chemo treatment as an outpatient. This would further my chances that the cancer would not come back. I was very disappointed to hear this news, but I knew it was the best thing for me. In August of 2012, I completed the chemo sessions at an outpatient UMHC center in Deerfield Beach, which was closer to my sister's home. This was the last chemo that I had throughout the cancer journey.

Dr. Temple did not want to place a wound vacuum or any other method for the wound to heal. He said he wanted it to heal naturally. Therefore, it took almost a year and a half for my wound to heal completely. This was after having a daily nurse to care for the wound, and later an additional wound nurse twice a week. In about September of 2013, the wound finally closed and healed.

Chemo had such an effect on my body overall. Of course, I lost weight, which I could not complain about because I needed that. However, one of the most difficult and challenging things that I had to go through in this journey was the frequent MRIs to monitor the status of my tumor.

In the beginning, they were done every few months. The most difficult thing about this process, as with the others, was lying on my back for hours. Unless you have experienced this procedure it would be hard to imagine the discomfort. After so many minutes my back would become as stiff as a board. My affected leg would often be in pain, as I had to always keep it still, and the technician sometimes strapped my legs down to help accomplish that goal.

I would pray so hard for God's help to endure this. I would also result to a similar method to counting sheep. I would listen to the loud sound of the machine and sometimes count the beats. Even though staff always gave me earphones and asked for my preferred music, the sound of the machine would drown out the music to a certain extent. Nevertheless, the sound of the gospel music and the lyrics helped take me through this torturous procedure.

Other times I would estimate the time that it would take for each song to play, which surprisingly helped the time to pass. In other words, I did everything possible to escape into another world while making it through it. The time was always longer than the technician said it would be. I remember one time my left foot started itching unbearably. I prayed to God to let it stop so I would not twitch or move and cause the test to be repeated. I know it was not my imagination, but I literally felt someone touch my foot as if they were scratching it. Whether it was an angel or not I do not know, but I thanked God for supernatural intervention.

Each MRI seemed to get harder and harder. On one occasion I could not do the regular MRI because I was in too much pain. Staff advised that it needed to be done in a hospital outpatient setting where pain medication could be administered through the IV. Therefore, I was admitted to the hospital for the procedure. I was totally surprised when the medical staff advised me that the MRI would take five hours to complete, and that I would be placed under anesthesia. I still suffer from the effects of that MRI due to the length of time my leg was held down.

As time passed, the MRIs became shorter as I no longer needed to have tests on both the femur and the knee. Also, the time span was expanded in which I needed to have MRIs every six months instead of a few months. As a cancer patient, every milestone is a moment to rejoice.

As of April 2017, I reached five years from the date of my cancer surgery. At that time, I had not returned to the cancer center for my six-month checkup with the oncologist, and for the MRI and chest x-ray.

Cancer Free

On June 13, 2017, I walked into my oncologist's office with confidence mixed with anxiety. Only someone who is a cancer survivor or in remission will fully understand this scenario.

Since I did not have an appointment in April; my anniversary month, this was the appointment that would confirm that I was a five-year cancer survivor. Many in the medical field prefer not to use that term at all for various reasons. For me, it was a welcome phrase after all I had been through.

Again, waiting was not easy. To some I may have looked fine on the outside. In the inside, I was filled with all kinds of emotions. The short wait in the lobby seemed like hours. Finally, I heard my name called and I sprung up from my seat. The preliminary vitals were taken by the nurse and as usual I was placed in the room to wait for the doctor.

Dr. Trent walked in with his usual welcoming smile. Throughout the journey, he has been a source of encouragement for me. His bedside manner continues to be great. As usual, he began by asking me how I was doing and other updates on my health. He then announced the words that I had been waiting to hear. "Your bloodwork and scans are fine." He said.

A big smile spread across my face and I had a big sigh of relief. It was hard to contain my happiness and excitement about what God had done for me. As I always do, I shared with my doctor that all praise belongs to God. It is Jesus Christ who has taken me through this journey thus far. I owe it all to the Lord Jesus Christ!

11
A Plan And Purpose For Your Life

Jeremiah 29:11
For I know the thoughts that I think toward you, saith the
LORD, thoughts of peace, and not of evil, to give you an ex-
pected end.

Over five years ago when I started on this cancer journey, I was
employed with the state of Florida-Department of Children and
Families, for thirty-one years. I considered myself a good employee and
had achieved a great deal through the ranks of the department. I had
worked in the Office of Client Relations for many years serving the public. My office handled general complaints about DCF services in the
Southern Region, which is Miami-Dade and Monroe County (The Keys).
My office also handled top customer concerns received via the DCF
Secretary's office, the Governor's office, legislative offices and other agen-
cies throughout the state.

When I learned of my cancer diagnosis, I had to take leave from my
job for the treatment plan that has been shared in this story. I had no idea
what the outcome would be, but I was trusting God that I would return to
work as soon as possible.

Once I began the treatments, it was obvious that I would be on leave for much longer than I had expected. When I first left work, my boss at that time offered me to work from home on a laptop. I accepted the offer with full intention of being able to do so. However, further into the treatment I realized this was impossible.

My cancer journey began in December of 2011. Chemo, surgery and other treatments lasted through August of 2012. I was unable to work during that time. As I previously said, my wound did not heal until about September 2013 and I remained using assistive devices during that time, up to the present. In 2012, I was still in pain and unable to sit for long periods of time. At work, I had a four-day work week schedule for a few years, working ten hours a day. This was not a situation that I could endure in my recuperation period.

Prior to this illness, I had felt the leading of the Holy Spirit to put in for my retirement and enroll in the state of Florida Deferred Retirement Option Program (DROP). Under this program, you stop earning service credit toward a future benefit, have your retirement benefit calculated at the time your DROP period begins and your monthly retirement benefits accumulate in the Florida Retirement System (FRS) Trust Fund earning interest while you continue to work for an FRS employer.

I thought long and hard about this decision to stop at the thirty-year mark, as my income would be limited after I completed the DROP program, since I would not meet the age requirement for Social Security benefits. I still felt led to take this option. Unbeknownst to me, I would later become ill at the thirty-one-year mark.

I had signed up for the DROP program in 2011. After being on sick leave from my job for months, I received a letter from my superiors that

I must return to work in October 2012. I was very concerned and disappointed as I was in no shape to return to work at that time. I was still in pain, still on crutches, and still unable to sit for long periods of time, etc. I prayed hard about what to do. I asked the Lord to guide me in making the right decision. I had some time to go before I would be completely retired, and could reap the full benefits of retirement.

I was never one to give up on anything or quit. I asked my superiors for a chance to work on the laptop at home, but they were unable to grant my request. I then asked for additional time to heal, and that request was also not granted. So, after much prayer I decided to end my employment with a total of 31 1/2 years of employment.

That was a very tough decision. I found consolation in knowing God had a plan for me. After all, he had brought me through the fire, had given me a miracle, and had extended my life. He had also led me through the wilderness. I had to believe the same God could and would provide for me. Indeed, God has done just that. Always put your total trust in God. He is God alone!

I have so many testimonies of God's goodness throughout my lifetime, but especially during this cancer journey. Remember earlier in my story I mentioned that I lost all my hair due to chemo. I was completely bald after the first round of chemo, which was only five days. After the final round of preventive chemo in August of 2012, as an outpatient, I lost the little hair that had grown back.

I and others were amazed at the fast growth of my hair. By my birthday in September 2013 my hair was medium length. I was wearing it natural. By the end of that year, my hair was full length. I use my hair as a testament of God's promise that I would be alright. I am a living testimony!

Through The Fire!

Here are some pictures taken between one year and a half and two years after chemo.

Hair styled by Joan Gray at Artistic Hair Salon
In Miami, Florida

What a mighty God we serve!
He is good and worthy to be praised!

Epilogue

At the time this book is being completed, I am still reporting to the Sylvester Comprehensive Cancer Center/ University of Miami Health Care for MRIs, chest x-rays and oncology appointments. During my last appointment in June, I was changed to one-year evaluations of my cancer free status.

Although I still walk with a limp, use an assistive device and have constant discomfort and pain in my right leg, I consider it nothing in comparison to what could have happened to me. I have seen other stories of people whose situation turned out different. I am grateful to my Jesus Christ for His healing and miraculous powers, not just through my cancer journey, but in my lifetime.

I still didn't realize just how blessed I was until I went for a follow-up visit to the cancer center. An older woman was sitting in the waiting room with me. She began to share her experience with sarcoma cancer. She said she had gone to several places within the state of Florida and other states seeking medical help and advice. She said when she first came to Sylvester, there was no doctor that could treat her properly.

She explained that after going many places she returned to Sylvester and was seeing the same doctor who had treated me. She spoke of how he had saved her life. I reflected on my first visit with Dr. Trent and how he was very new. I realized even more that God had placed me in the right place, and in the right hands to help me survive.

Never give up. Always believe God can and will come through. You may have to go through the fire, but you can come out without smelling like smoke. You must believe, have faith, and you must praise God during your trial or test. We serve a God who loves us and cares about our situations. Try him.

The children of Israel had seen God work miracles many times, yet they continued to forget what He had done. You were not led through the desert by a pillar of fire by night or by a cloud by day, but maybe you were about to make the wrong decision and the Holy Spirit gently whispered to you not to do it.

Maybe you were in danger of having an accident and the Lord led you in a different direction, or delayed your trip. Maybe you were about to give up, but a still quiet voice told you to keep going on. Maybe a friend or relative felt your need and provided it without you asking.

There are so many ways that the Lord guides, protects and shields us.

Psalm 32:8
I will instruct thee and teach thee in the way which thou shalt go:
I will guide thee with mine eye.

Isaiah 58:11
And the LORD shall guide thee continually, and satisfy thy soul in drought, and make fat thy bones: and thou shalt be like a watered garden, and like a spring of water, whose waters fail not. and satisfy thy soul in drought, and make fat thy bones: and thou shalt be like a watered garden, and like a spring of water, whose waters fail not.

I thank God for His grace and mercy. I praise Him for His goodness. I encourage you to always serve and honor Him. There is nobody like God.

He can bring you through the fire. Have faith. He can use others to inspire and encourage you while you are in the desert.

I did not write this book to provide any deep revelation or knowledge. My sole purpose is to share what the Lord has done in my life. Doctors are not God, but they too, can be used by the "Great I Am" to help you through. I am grateful that He has moved on my behalf, and has used medical staff to be instrumental in my survival.

There are several doctors who helped me through my cancer journey. I have obtained permission from these two doctors to name them in this book, and to display their picture. Dr. Jonathan Trent is my regular Oncologist housed at the Sylvester Comprehensive Cancer Center, in Miami.

These pictures were taken with him during a follow-up visit in May of 2016.

Me with Dr. Jonathan Trent, M.D.

Me sitting outside of Sylvester Comprehensive Cancer Center
with the statue of Philanthropist Harcourt Sylvester Jr.
(May 2016)

Dr. H. Thomas Temple, is the Orthopedic
Oncologist who lead the surgery to remove the tumor from my leg. He has since left
the University of Miami to take a position at Nova
Southeastern University, in Ft. Lauderdale, Florida. He has
also opened a new practice at Mercy Hospital in Miami.

Dr. H. Thomas Temple, M.D.